T0313465

BECOMING MEN

BECOMING MEN

Black Masculinities in a
South African Township

Malose Langa

WITS UNIVERSITY PRESS

Published in South Africa by:
Wits University Press
1 Jan Smuts Avenue
Johannesburg 2001

www.witspress.co.za

Copyright © Malose Langa 2020
Published edition © Wits University Press 2020
Cover image © 2019 Siphosihle Mkhwanazi | DALRO

First published 2020

http://dx.doi.org.10.18772/12020045676

978-1-77614-567-6 (Paperback)
978-1-77614-571-3 (Hardback)
978-1-77614-568-3 (Web PDF)
978-1-77614-569-0 (EPUB)
978-1-77614-570-6 (Mobi)

All rights reserved. No part of this publication may be reproduced, stored in a retrieval
system, or transmitted in any form or by any means, electronic, mechanical, photocopying,
recording or otherwise, without the written permission of the publisher, except in
accordance with the provisions of the Copyright Act, Act 98 of 1978.

Project manager: Elaine Williams
Copyeditor: Alison Lowry
Proofreader: Alison Lockhart
Indexer: Elaine Williams
Cover design: Hybrid Creative
Typesetter: Lumina Datamatics
Typeset in 11.5 point Crimson

For all the young men interviewed in the book

Contents

Acknowledgements

Finally, this book is published! It has taken me many years of procrastinating but also of thinking deeply and critically about young masculinities in South Africa and the world as a whole. This book would not have been possible without the support and assistance of the many people I met, spoke to and whose work I read. To all of you, I wish to say thank you for directly and indirectly enriching my mind and guiding me to complete this book.

I would like to thank my colleagues at the Centre for the Study of Violence and Reconciliation (CSVR), where my journey into the world of research was born. At CSVR I met brilliant researchers such as Bronwyn Harris, Sasha Gear, David Bruce, Hugo van der Merwe, Themba Masuku and many others. Special thanks also to Nomfundo Mogapi, Melissa Hunter, Marivic Garcia-Mall, Sonto Mbatha, Kindiza Ngubeni, Modiege Merafe, Tsamme Mfundisi, Steven Rebello, Selby Xiwna, Tsholo Sesanga and Sophie Mulaudzi for the support you provided when I started as an intern at CSVR, and as I worked my way through the ranks to the level of associate senior researcher.

This achievement would not have been possible without my mentor, teacher and motivator, the late Boitumelo 'Malome' Kekana. Petles, you will get your copy of the book when we meet on the other side. I owe this to you, Malome!

I wish also to express my utmost appreciation to my PhD supervisor and mentor, Professor Gill Eagle, for providing invaluable support and guidance throughout the process of completing this book. Many thanks for all your in-depth, detailed and constructive editorial and scholarly comments. Thanks for the time you made to read my countless emails and to provide feedback on draft after draft. Much appreciated!

Thank you to all the young men I interviewed for the research project, which has been shaped into this book It has been a long journey. I met you as young high school boys between the ages of 13 and 18 and you are now young men aged between 23 and 28 years. Thanks very much for giving your precious time to take photos and participate in the interviews, for allowing me to enter your private worlds and for telling me about the difficulties that young black boys and men face in post-apartheid South Africa. I hope your life stories will enrich other boys' lives and serve as a lesson for young black men in South Africa and beyond.

Thanks to all my colleagues in the Department of Psychology at the University of the Witwatersrand (Wits), especially Garth Stevens, Daleen Alexander, Vinitha Jithoo, Tanya Swart, Peace Kiguwa, Hugo Canham and Brett Bowman, for all your support and words of encouragement to finish this book project. Thanks to all my Master's students (especially MACC students) who worked with me on various research projects on masculinities. Many thanks to Lerato Moroeng for helping me with queries regarding my research budget, travelling arrangements and other logistics. I wish to express my appreciation to Professor Karl von Holdt for his inspiration and motivation in directing me to other research projects on violence. Thank you also to Professor Kopano Ratele at the Medical Research Council (MRC) for the opportunity to be involved in your research projects on masculinities. I hope the insight you shared with me is well represented in this book.

The research project was funded by the South Africa-Netherlands Research Programme on Alternatives in Development (SANPAD), DST-NRF Centre of Excellence in Human Development, the National Research Foundation (NRF) and the African Doctoral Dissertation Research Fellowship (ADDRF) offered by the African Population and Health Research Center (APHRC) in partnership with the International

Development Research Center (IDRC) and the Ford Foundation. For helping me to get funding for this project, I would like to express my gratitude to Professor Graham Lindegger at the University of KwaZulu-Natal, as well as to Caroline Kabiru and Chima Izugbara at the APHRC in Kenya. I wish to express my appreciation to Shireen Hassim for financially supporting my sabbatical leave, through funds from the Mellon Foundation, to be a visiting scholar at Stony Brook University, New York, USA. Thanks to Professor Michael Kimmel at Stony Brook's Center for the Study of Men and Masculinities for hosting me as I completed this book project. It was a privilege to sit in on your lectures on sex and sexuality, and I gained much insight out of these engagements with you and your students.

Thank you to Stephen Frosh for allowing me to be a visiting scholar at the department of Psychosocial Studies at Birkbeck College, University of London, UK. I learned so much in attending your lectures on psychoanalysis and masculinities, which helped me to better conceptualise my research.

Thank you Lee Smith for your thoroughness in proofreading and editing the first draft of this book. Your ability to spot and track all missing sources was amazing.

I also wish to express my appreciation to the Wits Press team (especially Roshan Cader and Elaine Williams) for all your support and words of encouragement in publishing this book. Special words of appreciation to my editor Alison Lowry for helping me simplify academic arguments into something easy to read.

Lastly, I wish to express my appreciation to all my cousins, aunts, uncles and other relatives, especially my mom Velly Langa, and my sister Sada Langa and late brother Louis Langa. A special thank you to my aunts Lydia Sekhu, Violet Matlou and Constance Totone Kgatla, and my uncle Professor ST Kgatla, for your support with my undergraduate studies, which enabled me to reach this level of my career, as well as to my cousin Mmankosi for all your motivation and belief in me. I also dedicate this book to all my friends, especially Benji (Kuka), Venon,

Kevin Naidu, Mahlaba (Kgogo), Ngoako, Lenin (Phistos), Brian, Marifi, Sima, Benny (Sprongolo), Nana and Malesela (Moja).

This book is also dedicated to my wife (Princess), and my two little girls Paballo and Atlegang, who had to endure my absence while I focused on it. I hope this book will make changes for you as young girls and allow you to grow up in a world free of violence perpetrated by boys and men.

1 | What Makes a Man a Man?

In 2007 I began a study of a group of adolescent boys growing up in the South African township of Alexandra. Alex, as it is known, was established in 1912 and as such is one of the oldest townships in the country. It is situated just north-east of Johannesburg, close to the affluent suburb of Sandton, and the majority of those who live there are working-class people. The place is overcrowded and under-serviced, and poverty, violence and crime are rife.

My subjects (participants) were all schoolboys between the ages of 13 and 18 at the time I began to get to know them. The boys were from different schools. Some knew each other but were not close friends. My plan was to conduct a longitudinal study, with the main aim being to explore how adolescent boys negotiate their transition to adulthood in the context of a township, and in doing so observe how they understand what it means to be a 'real' man and whether definitions of masculinity might be static, changing or fluid. I followed them over a period of close on 12 years (2007 to 2018) so that by the time of the conclusion of my study they were all young adults between 24 and 28 years old.

After the first phase of data collection in 2007, I then followed 12 of the boys over the next nearly 12 years, conducting between 6 and 18 individual follow-up interviews with each of them. Eleven of the 12 completed high school (one dropped out in Grade 11) and four completed tertiary-level diplomas. At the time of writing, 10 of the participants were working, one was unemployed and one was in prison.

The field of study – boys and masculinity – is not new. Broadly, it may be characterised as the study of male experience, but this varies according to a specific context and across socio-historical-cultural formations. What is relatively new, however, is what ongoing contemporary research in many parts of the world has revealed. This is that the stereotyped ideas that have dictated what it means to be a man are changing. Certain groups of boys in the world today are not engaging in risk-taking and other problematic behaviours as part of constructing their masculine identities. Instead they are promoting different kinds of masculine ideals. More emphasis, for example, is being placed on academic success and long-term career goals; and ways of relating to girls and other boys in a more egalitarian manner.

I wanted to explore how much of an echo these international findings there was here, on home soil in South Africa, and, more specifically, when it came to black boys in a township environment.

Relying on stereotypes of race, gender and class, many people tend to associate young black males from townships such as Alex with crime and violence. I wanted to test these assumptions.

Over the last few years, there have been a number of South African studies on masculinities, many of them focusing on problems associated with young black boys and men, ranging from poor academic performance to gangsterism, gender-based violence, HIV/AIDS, substance abuse and violent crime. The dominant discourse that has emerged out of these studies is that young black boys and men are more likely than young men of other races to engage in risk-taking and violent behaviours.

As a researcher, I have an ongoing and applied academic interest in working with at-risk youth. This included some years back working with juvenile offenders in prison as an intern counselling psychologist at the Centre for the Study of Violence and Reconciliation (CSVR). During my work with juvenile offenders, questions about prison masculinities arose, more particularly through the stories that many young offenders shared with me and my colleagues. Juvenile offenders' stories entailed notions of violent masculinities, which were defined by some as the key markers of being a 'real' man, and how these practices led them to prison through their involvement in violent crimes. I was troubled as a young intern to hear these detailed, often gory stories of armed robberies with aggravating circumstances, including cases of assault, murder and rape.

My curiosity about what it means to be a man started at that point.

How does the notion of manhood contribute to violence and violent crime? And, in the context of offenders awaiting trial or serving time, how does this notion of manhood contribute to violence and gangster-ism in prison?[1]

I needed to go further back, to the question: What makes a man a man?

How do boys construct their masculine identities?

It seemed to me that there was a major gap in terms of our knowl-edge of the psychosocial processes involved in what it means to be a 'boy'. This was the gap I wanted to be able, in part, to fill.

I wanted to explore how boys or young men develop and live differ-ent versions of hegemonic and alternative masculinities, as reflected in their everyday conversations. A longitudinal study would be especially interesting, I decided, because it would offer a longer-term perspective on many of the core and related issues I hoped would emerge. Most masculinities studies involve only one or two interviews, whereas I would be conducting between 4 and 12 over a period of years.

The questions I began to compile helped me to formulate my approach.

What motivates boys in constructing their identities? What moti-vates them to behave in a particular manner? How do they feel about their masculinities? What are the emotional costs of occupying certain mascu-line positions over others? What are the feelings and emotions associated with the positions boys occupy as part their masculine identities? What are the voices of resistance? Is it possible for alternative voices to emerge and, if so, how do they emerge? What informs their emergence?

These questions also resonated with my own lived experiences as a black teenager. When I was a herdboy in the rural areas of Limpopo province (Mapela Village, Ga-Matopa) I, too, was exposed to various pressures to behave in a particular manner as a way of confirming that I was a 'real' boy. One such pressure was fist fighting to prove who was a 'real' man, while other risk-taking behaviours included drinking, smoking and sniffing glue or benzene with my friends. These behaviours were popular at the time and it was commonly expected that many teenagers would indulge in some or all of them.

The construction of hegemonic masculinity has been found to be a key element in risk-taking behaviours, but there have been some studies that have shown that young black men are able to promote different kinds of masculine ideals,[2] ones that do not envisage risk-taking and other problematic behaviours as part of constructing their masculine identities. Despite the associated difficulties, they are able to reject and resist pressure from their male peers to comply with dominant or hegemonic masculine practices. It has also been found that they can experience mixed feelings about their masculine identities.[3]

In the context of a black South African township, however, currently we know relatively little about how young black boys construct their masculine identities, what motivates them, and how they feel about their masculinities, especially alternative masculinities. A psychosocial theory may help us to further explore implications of living out a particular form of masculinity in a township environment.

Together with how masculinities are constructed, therefore, I also wanted my study to listen for voices of alternative masculinities – those that are non-risk taking, non-sexist and not harmful to self and others – and hear how adolescent boys in Alexandra felt about such alternative masculinities. The interviews, as these reflected their daily lives and the daily struggles they encountered, I believed, would give me useful answers.

*

I started the research with 32 boys in the group. As part of my methodology, I gave them disposable cameras, which many of them were excited about as at the time very few people had cell phones with cameras. Using cameras allowed me to develop a close emotional relationship with each boy in the study, as I had to make repeated visits to their schools and keep contact with each boy to give and collect the cameras. In retrospect, using photography was a novel and creative way of researching black masculinities because the boys were free to take photos of things they felt truly represented their identities, lives, wishes and fantasies about the future. It was also exciting for me to look at and analyse the photographic images the boys took. Some of the photos showed me that a lot of reflection and introspection had gone into the taking of the pictures, and into what the images meant and represented to the boys.

During the second longitudinal phase of the study, the boys (who were now young men) used their cell phones rather than disposable cameras to take photos representing their lives. In the follow-up interviews they were encouraged to share at least four photos that significantly represented their life story at the time of each interview. The photos taken during this period represented a major shift from adolescence to being a young man.

Both the individual and group interviews at the outset were conducted on the boys' school premises; for the follow-up interviews some of the participants preferred that I go to their homes. As trust between us was gradually established and the boys matured, they felt more comfortable about volunteering information in our private conversations reflecting self-doubt, sadness around certain areas of their lives, and misgivings about some of the commonly accepted portrayals of their boyhood. The rapport between us was well developed and allowed for in-depth disclosure of intimate material.

My interview style was informal and relaxed, and all the interviews were tape-recorded and transcribed for analysis. In addition, I always had

field notebooks in which I wrote my personal reflections about each interview and recorded my impressions and feelings (for example, whether it
was an 'easy' or 'difficult' interview, whether there were any unexpected
aspects in the interview, my own feelings about points made in the interview and so on). Writing field notes helped me gain more insight into the
inner worlds of the boys as well as into my own feelings and emotions.
For example, was I, as a young black researcher who had once also been a
teenager, over-identifying with the emerging material or the boys' views
in the interviews? How did I experience these boys and how did they experience me? How did they feel about talking to me and vice versa? What
kinds of feelings did they evoke in me and how did I handle these feelings?

Two important factors that I needed to take into account were those
of my race and my gender. Did my identity as a young black male play
any role in my interaction with these boys? Did they see me as a distant or a caring male figure? My field notes included my observations
about how the boys responded to me and my questions. Many commented that most of my questions were fine, but that the questions on
sex and sexuality were a bit difficult, especially when they were still in
high school. Talking about sex was a sensitive subject for some of them.
However, not all the boys found it difficult to talk about sex and sexuality. Some answered these questions in detail and boasted about the
number of girls they had sex with. Others were clearly performing in
these interviews, especially the group sessions, to show that they were
'real' macho boys who had multiple girlfriends.

It seemed that talking 'man to man' in the interviews made many of
the boys feel relaxed, because I showed an interest in their stories and
was not judgemental about their risk-taking behaviours, such as having
sex with multiple partners, smoking, drinking and using illegal drugs.
There was a sense of camaraderie and brotherhood in many of the interviews. One boy said, 'I have never spoken to my brothers like the way I
spoke with you.' Another said, 'I know that you are also a male. You also
grew up. You were also once my age. You were also a teenager. Stuff like
that. That made me talk more and feel free and comfortable.'

The interviews clearly evoked a range of feelings in the participants. For example, some expressed the wish that their parents, especially their fathers, and older brothers, were more open to discussing intimate issues such as sex, girlfriends, HIV and AIDS, and their involvement in risk-taking behaviours. Others reflected that it was easy to talk to me, especially about their intimate relationships and personal challenges, because they knew 'as a man I would understand their positions or things that were frustrating them'. Given this view, I had to be objective to ensure that I did not collude with problematic masculine discourses that may have been oppressive or patriarchal. For instance, there was a time when one of the young men was experiencing relationship difficulties that might potentially have led him to behave violently towards his partner. We reflected on some of his frustrations without any judgement in order for him to gain insight into his behaviour.

Conversations were also held about the problem of gender-based violence, including the #MenAreTrash social media campaign that arose during the period following the murder of a young woman by her male partner, and many other incidents that happened subsequently. Many of the young men vehemently rejected the notion that 'men are trash' but acknowledged that it was a problem that men needed to tackle as they were the main perpetrators of violence against women. One study participant proposed that other young men beyond the reach of this particular research project also needed to be given the opportunity to talk about men and violence against women. His view was that such public dialogues, if managed constructively, would help to reduce this problem in the country.

My self-awareness throughout the research process was useful to me. I also used these feelings to better understand the boys' emotional concerns and the difficulties they encountered in their daily lives.

My relationships with the 12 boys who became the core of my research group differed significantly from boy to boy. Some I became very close to, and my bond with them grew stronger and stronger as we continued to meet individually over a long period of time.

My observation was that these participants became less guarded in their responses and became open about sharing with me even their deepest feelings. I bore witness to emotions – of hurt, shame, humiliation, for example – which I understood would not be easily shared with anyone and I treated these intimate sessions with respect. As they left boyhood behind I had in-depth discussions about various challenges in the young men's personal lives, things such as the loss of a child, loss of a job, unanticipated fatherhood, imprisonment (in the case of one of them) and difficulties they were experiencing in their intimate relationships. I used our meetings as opportunities for them to process these difficulties and to try and assist them in that process. Some of them even called me to request that we meet and talk and I greatly valued this demonstration of trust.

Our interactions were generally informal. Over a decade or so we met in coffee shops, pubs, restaurants or Ga-Maimane *chesanyama* in Alex.[4] Some I visited at their workplaces or homes, while others came to my office on a number of occasions. By this stage they were all using fancy cell phones to take and send their photos – the days of disposable cameras were dead and buried! – and we would often laugh about the fact that they had used disposable cameras when we started our journey together. Nevertheless those disposables were very useful at the time.

In research terms the repeated interviews helped me to gain invaluable insight into the tensions and contradictions that young black men encounter and how they try to resolve them.

During the research process, I also had to reflect on my own position and the power relations between these young men and myself. All of them knew that I was a psychologist and lecturer at the University of the Witwatersrand and that the research project I was doing was intended for my PhD thesis. My professional background automatically gave me a position of power because I was seen as an educated person whom they could rely on. As a researcher, I always needed to be aware of this position of power in my interaction with these boys/young men. When they were still in high school, all the boys called me Mr Langa (or sir), perhaps in some ways locating or relating to me as similar to a teacher in their environment. Later, after I got my PhD, which they were informed about, some started calling me Dr Langa. I believe it was out of respect and perhaps some idealisation that they all used my surname, Langa, as opposed to my first name, Malose, which would have been a more casual form of address and what I would have preferred.

As I conducted interviews, formal and informal, listened to and participated in conversations with my group of Alex boys, they revealed to me what I had hoped they would: how young boys construct, protect and defend their masculinities and create new ones. This is in line with Raewyn Connell's argument that masculinities are constantly being protected and defended, breaking and being recreated. All masculinities compete to be the best.

Gaining a better understanding of practices of masculinity in terms of boys' and young men's everyday experiences in a township such as Alexandra (and understanding the broader township commonalities in different regions in South Africa) gives us a vantage point for insights that are both unique and of value. The stories of the young black adolescent boys who participated in my study, as they transitioned to young adulthood in the new South Africa, took shape into this book, *Becoming Men*. The research project was intended to make a useful contribution to the growing body of work on masculinities studies. Alongside this, however, is my hope that its findings will be used by teachers, researchers and policy makers in South Africa – and further afield – to develop public policies and campaigns that promote healthy alternative constructions of masculinity aimed at reducing high-risk behaviours associated with hegemonic masculinity.

2 | Reshaping Masculinities – Understanding the Lives of Adolescent Boys

Multiple studies have already been done and ideas of 'alternative' constructions of masculinity, based on the premise that masculinity is fluid, multiple and flexible,[1] continue to be explored and examined, both in South Africa and abroad. In contemporary research masculinities are plural constructs and should be considered as belonging in fixed ways to all men. Some of the British and Australian researchers who have led the way in focusing on young masculinities are Stephen Frosh, Ann Phoenix and Rob Pattman, as well as Raewyn Connell, Wayne Martino, Jon Swain, Emma Renold, Christian Haywood and Máirtín Mac an Ghaill. It was these views and voices, as well as those of other South African researchers, that stimulated my exploration of the theme with adolescent boys in Alexandra township. I wanted to see whether the same positive elements and signs of masculinity, or masculinities, which do not subscribe to the stereotype, as findings were showing, were as evident when it came to the typical 'township boy'.

Critical masculinity studies have gained momentum in South Africa in recent years. After 1994, added impetus came in part from an attempt to understand how the politics of gender intersected with issues of transition and constitutional democracy, which enshrines basic human rights principles, including gender equality. Leading figures in this field of enquiry in South Africa include Robert Morrell, Clive Glaser, Mark Hunter, Jacklyn Cock, Gill Eagle, Garth Stevens, Graham Lindegger,

Linda Richter, Lisa Vetten, Rachel Jewkes, Kopano Ratele, Tamara Shefer, Deevia Bhana and Mzi Nduna.

Researchers and scholars now broadly agree that masculinity is not static and stagnant, but can and does change. Significantly, these changes reveal that not all boys are the same. Theorists like Connell, Morrell, Frosh and colleagues have moved away from masculinity as a single construct: 'an area of agreement emerged among North America, British and Australian writers in recent years that we no longer talk about masculinity but about masculinities'.[2] Many researchers now use the plural form 'masculinities' to acknowledge the variety of interpretive forms that masculinity can take. Within the refocus there are different kinds of masculine identities, which are ranked hierarchically, with some forms being subordinated, complicit and/or marginalised.[3] In terms of South Africa, Morrell confirms: 'there is no one, typical South African masculinity', but rather different masculinities.

The notion of hegemonic masculinity in context

In order fully to understand why this research is particularly relevant and interesting, one needs first to grasp the basic meaning of what is meant by 'hegemonic masculinity', which became a widely used and popularised concept in studies of men and masculinity.

The concept of hegemony was derived from the work of Italian sociologist Antonio Gramsci and his analysis of class relations.[4] Gramsci, a Marxist, used the term to critique the power the bourgeoisie had over the working-class masses in a capitalist economic system. He claimed that the bourgeoisie used their political power to control and dominate the working class and sustain a leading position in social life. The idea of hegemony was used to capture both structural and ideological or discursive dominance within certain sets of relations, pertaining in this instance primarily to class position and power.

The term 'hegemonic masculinity' first emerged two decades ago, proposed by Australian sociologist Raewyn Connell in reports on a field study of social inequality in Australian high schools, which in itself had evolved out of a related conceptual discussion on the making of masculinities in Australian labour politics. In coining the term, Connell was applying the principle of hegemony in the context of how some men use power to maintain control and domination over women and, interestingly, also over sub-groups of men. She defined the term as 'the configuration of gender practice which embodies the currently accepted answer to the problem of the legitimacy of patriarchy, which guarantees (or is taken to guarantee) the dominant position of men and the subordination of women'.[5] Moreover, hegemonic masculinity refers to the prevailing dominant cultural stereotype of masculinity in a society, community or group. Take, for example, the dominant view in many societies of men as brave, strong, aggressive and resilient. Another dominant cultural stereotype could be one that suggests that a 'real man' is a male person who is able to support a wife and children by earning a steady income, has the ability to face and solve problems or to demand sexual intercourse with multiple partners.[6]

In general, hegemonic versions of masculinity maintain that gender is not negotiable. They do not accept evidence from feminist and other sources that the relationships between men and women are in many aspects politically and socially constructed.[7] In these versions patriarchy and the oppression of women are justified as part of culture and biology, and as reflecting the 'natural order' of relationships. They are characterised not only by male domination over women, but also by domination over other men, especially gay men. According to Demetrakis Demetriou, hegemonic masculinity should thus be understood as both 'hegemony over women' and 'hegemony over subordinate masculinities'.[8]

Over time, some men and boys began to feel the burden of being constrained and defined by this construction or ideal of masculinity. These men, and feminist women, agreed that the main enemies were the social roles or set of expectations into which boys and men were forced by conventional ideas of what a man should be. In part as a result of this shift, criticisms were also raised about the construct's failure to acknowledge that the categories of hegemony – subordination, complicity and marginalisation – are not always easily distinguishable; neither are they fixed in place. Some boys and men may occupy all these positions concurrently or they may vacillate between them, depending on their context.[9] Hegemonic relations in any society involve a constant contest and struggle for power and visibility, complexities that Connell did not take into account in her early writings. It must be taken into account that she developed the notion of hegemonic masculinity while she was still rooted in understanding the class politics of the Australian capitalist economic system and its impact on men as partners and fathers. Since then, Connell has made substantial changes to the concept. She now recognises the diversity, fluidity and multiplicity of masculinities, including hegemonic and counter-hegemonic positions.[10]

Boys are constantly acting to maintain or occupy multiple and even opposing positions in their lived experiences,[11] thereby illustrating that relationships in respect of masculinity are non-static. As Demetriou asserts, 'it is an illusion to think of hegemonic masculinity as a closed, coherent and unified identity'.[12] Rather it is characterised by the constant process of negotiation, translation and reconfiguration in order to adapt to new historical periods and contexts. Thus, both within groups and in individuals, shifts between hegemonic and counter-hegemonic positions may take place very quickly, indicating coexistence and contestation. What versions of masculinity dominate or occupy a prominent position in any circumstance can also be subject to change. It is therefore important not to consider hegemonic masculinity as a single notion.

South African researchers Morrell, Jewkes and Lindegger have noted that the term tends to be universally and rigidly used in masculinity studies, without any recognition of the influence of other dynamic factors – race and class differences, for example – and how these might play out.[13] Ratele takes this criticism further by highlighting the term's limitations in fully explaining male homicide in South Africa.[14]

He argues that, despite their position of subordination in township spaces, some poor young black boys victimise each other. Through perpetrating violence, they then occupy a hegemonic position within this position of subordination. However, at the same time, they occupy a marginal position compared to other boys in terms of class or race.

This demonstrates how the notion of hegemony intersects with other contextual factors such as race, class and culture and I was especially mindful of this when doing my research in Alexandra township in the many interviews I conducted with my group of adolescents as they matured into young men. Multiple factors, as I discovered through their first-hand accounts, influence young black boys to develop certain masculine voices or behave in a particular manner. At times I felt I needed to delve deeper, as I became more aware of the social and internal contradictions and psychological processes related to what it means to be a 'real' boy, as articulated by them in our conversations that pertained to different versions of masculinity in the context of their lived experiences.

The concept of hegemonic masculinity remains highly influential in masculinity studies despite the criticisms that have been levelled against it. It remains useful for understanding social positioning and the ways in which certain expressions of masculinity become dominant, legitimated and celebrated, while others are rendered less legitimate. It continues to inspire many masculinity studies, including my own examination of adolescent boys' involvement in certain risk-taking behaviours.

Risk-taking behaviours of school-age boys

Adolescence is a period in which boys experiment with sex, substance taking and other potentially risky behaviours in order to consolidate their masculine identities. Many academic sources emphasise that adolescent boys, in particular, are at risk of a range of psychosocial problems.[15] One major concern is over their deteriorating academic performance – more boys than girls of this age group perform poorly when it comes to their school grades.[16] Elaine Unterhalter, for example, found that more boys repeat both primary and secondary grades than girls.[17] Furthermore, the number of girls entering higher education is slowly and increasingly exceeding that of the number of boys.[18] Some researchers view this situation as indicating that boys are in a 'crisis' situation, which fuels the growing public concern about the plight of boys in schools.[19] Boys are more likely to be labelled 'troublemakers' in terms of truancy, discipline problems, suspensions and expulsions. Many of these problems in both primary and secondary schools have been linked with the expression and practices of masculinities, which encourage casual treatment of schoolwork, defiance of adult authority, missing classes, and the social disapproval of boys who put emphasis on academic success.[20]

It is important to bear in mind that power and struggle are often central to the experience of masculine identities and the cost of pursuing an appropriate masculine identity can be heavy for adolescent boys, who often find themselves struggling to live up to expectations of being a 'real' man. Research has illustrated that boys experience pressure to perform certain scripts of masculinity at a very young age, usually through displays of hardiness, prowess in sport and risk-taking behaviours.[21] Boys who do not comply with these practices are called derogatory names such as 'losers', 'nerds' and *yimvu* (Zulu word for sheep).[22] No boy child wants to be called any of these derogatory names. In fact, this may be a source of violence among boys in order to prove that one is not a *lekwala* (Sotho word for coward) but brave and fearless. Ratele argues that the need among young boys to demonstrate fearlessness heightens their vulnerability to or perpetration of violence. The pressure not to reveal fear and anxiety, he says, pushes young boys to never walk away from a fight and to show bravado by fighting back. This explains why so many young boys dominate crime statistics as both victims and perpetrators of various forms of violence.

Studies based on the work of Kopano Ratele, David Bruce and Steffen Jensen describe how some young boys see engaging in violence as a form of asserting their masculine identity.[23] In his book *Gang Town*, a study of gang culture on the Cape Flats, Don Pinnock says that the more brutal and daring the violence a boy commits, the more respect he gets in the eyes of his male peers. Elaine Salo provides empirical evidence in her work with young adolescent boys in the Western Cape of how many learn about gang practices at a young age. Rich examples are provided of how gangs perform certain rituals and school new members to comply with traditional gang codes. Some gang codes involve 'spilling blood' (for example, injuring or even killing someone or committing a violent crime) as part of the initiation.[24] After performing a ritual, a new gang member is tattooed, using a needle and ink made from hot, melted rubber. The new initiate is expected to endure the pain without complaining or crying.[25] As part of this rite of passage, new gang members are also expected to take on the ethos of the gang and be prepared to die for the gang in any gang warfare. Gang fights over turf, community resources, women and the drug markets are very common. These fights also involve the masculine performance of fearlessness and bravery.[26] Don Pinnock and Jonny Steinberg, respectively in their books (*Gang Town* and *The Number*), discuss how the prison gang culture has infiltrated the streets of the Cape Flats, where young boys on the outside align themselves with prison gangs such as the 26s, 27s and 28s. This is one explanation for the ever increasing number of gang-related fights and killings on the Cape Flats and in the surrounding communities.

Irvin Kinnes found that young boys on the Cape Flats join gangs because membership provides them with increased opportunities and access to desirable material possessions, such as expensive cars and clothing, as well as to women.[27] In addition, gang members enjoy a certain respect and status. They are seen as role models for many young men, especially in disadvantaged communities, because they epitomise the image of a particular kind of success. This celebration of criminalised masculinity among young male South Africans in some sectors of the population directly contributes to the incidents of violent crime that are reported daily in our media and in crime statistics.

How these dynamics of gang masculinities play themselves out was one of the important things I explored with the focus group of young boys in Alex as I interviewed them over the 12-year period.

*

The HIV and AIDS pandemic has raised many questions about the sexual behaviour of young men. In South Africa, scholars have noted how dominant masculinities tend to shape young men's violent control over women, and their celebration of multiple partners.[28] Katharine Wood and Rachel Jewkes in their work, as well as Deevia Bhana and Rob Pattman, found that many young boys also boast about the number of girlfriends they have and their ability to have sex with all of them.[29] In a study of masculinities and multiple sex partners in parts of KwaZulu-Natal, Mark Hunter described men who had sex with multiple partners as *amasoka* (from the Zulu word for boyfriends), adding that their status was celebrated by other men in their communities.[30]

For some young men, a relationship or sex is about quantity rather than quality. Young boys often ask one another how many girlfriends they have, and how often they have sex with them; some go so far as betting about who can sleep with the most women. Young boys achieve status, prestige and popularity among their peers by having multiple partners and through publicly demonstrating or proclaiming this. Boys also feel entitled to have full penetrative sex with females when and how they want it, particularly when they have spent money on them, such as buying them drinks at a shebeen or pub or taking them out to movies and buying them sweets or chocolates.[31] In this context, successful masculinity is centred on young boys' ability to control their sexual partners and to have sex with them on their own terms. Regarding the discourse around the male sexual drive, sex is presented as a 'masculine or physical need', while girls' and women's desires are barely recognised. Boys feel entitled to initiate a sexual encounter, but young girls are denied this privilege. Girls who initiate sexual encounters or carry condoms are labelled *difebe* (sluts), loose, whores or prostitutes.[32]

In relationships, it is boys who largely control the sexual activity, including the use or non-use of condoms. It seems condoms are reserved for casual encounters (one-night stands, for example) or 'secret lovers' (cherries).[33] In this respect, hegemonic masculinity is saturated with associations of a dominant, active and promiscuous heterosexuality. In trusting or steady relationships, condoms tend to be abandoned after a few months once the female is considered *regte* (a steady girlfriend). Thereafter it becomes extremely difficult to reintroduce condoms, as this implies either that one has a sexually transmitted disease or that one mistrusts one's partner.

Girls commonly need to be submissive in 'love affairs' or they risk being beaten up. Some young boys claim that violence against girlfriends is a sign of love and also a legitimate means of instilling discipline in girlfriends who are considered to be stubborn and defiant.[34] Numerous studies in South Africa show that many women (including young girls) are likely to experience some form of violence during their lifetime – sexual harassment, rape and emotional and/or physical abuse.[35] Rachel Jewkes and her colleagues assert that violence against girls and women is a major public health problem in South Africa. Pumla Gqola describes the culture of rape as 'a South African nightmare' that haunts us daily, with perpetrators getting younger and younger and more violent in their actions.[36] Some, according to Ratele, especially young boys and men as part of their resistance to changing gender relations, argue that women are not the only victims and that boys and men are victims of gender-based violence too. This despite the fact that statistically men are the main perpetrators of violence against girls and women. Boys and men often raise their resistant voices on social media during campaigns such as '16 Days of Activism for No Violence against Women and Children'. Some of these voices were also raised sharply during more recent public social media campaigns such as #MenAreTrash or #TotalShutdown in response to incidents of violence against women.

Drawing on patriarchal attitudes, boys and young men see themselves as superior to young girls and women. These are attitudes that young boys learn from an early age. In their school-based work interviews, Shefer and her colleagues provided illustrative examples of how, in group interviews, schoolboys asserted the need for men to be heads of households and voiced their expectations of women doing household chores because their husbands had paid *lobola* (bridewealth).[37] Their dominant view was that women who do not comply with these cultural norms risk being beaten up. Some boys seem to think it is their birthright, given their gender as males, to oppress and abuse women.

However, some young girls and women today are defying male control over them by also engaging in relationships with more than one partner, deciding who to date, and demanding that sex be on their terms. As a result, some young boys complain bitterly about their inability to retain the interest of 'beautiful' girls and women who prefer to date sugar daddies or 'blessers' (men who are already working, drive flashy cars and who can afford to buy them expensive gifts, including taking trips outside the country). This makes it difficult for young boys and men to have girlfriends. Their inability to provide the lifestyle a 'blesser' can offer may challenge the development of a successful masculine identity and compromise their status in the eyes of their male peers. In this context, successful masculinity is associated with economic power; those without wealth feel they are not 'man enough' or are emasculated due to their inability to fulfil the ideals of what a 'real' man should be. Here, successful hegemonic masculinity appears to be associated with both heterosexuality (and sexual prowess) and access to wealth, material possessions and resources.

In my interviews over time with the Alex boys I was interested, therefore, not only in the kinds of social patterns, exchanges and labels that had been identified in other related research, but also how these boys positioned themselves in terms of their own class and access to girls as potential girlfriends and related sexual practices in the relationships they formed, both as schoolboys and later as young adults.

*

Another social ill associated with being male is the problem of substance abuse. Although women also smoke, drink and use drugs, the rates are much higher among young South African men. The statistics released every year by the South African Community Epidemiology Network on Drug Use show this pattern.[38] It seems that many young males experiment with alcohol and other drugs at a young age to consolidate their emerging masculine identities. During this phase of experimentation, young men who drink large amounts of alcohol without vomiting or passing out, smoke excessively and take hard drugs are seen as clever or strong (skhokho) by many of their male peers. For these young men, the pressure to use drugs or alcohol is linked to proving their manliness and winning status and the admiration of their male peer group.[39]

The same pressure also influences young men to be involved in risk-taking behaviours such as reckless driving, including drinking and driving.[40] Driving dangerously is a way of constructing oneself as masculine. According to Connell, injury on the road is the leading cause of sudden death for boys and men. The World Report on Road Traffic Injury Prevention indicates that drinking and driving is the leading cause of death globally among young people.[41] In South Africa, the number of road accidents involving young men is alarming. A 2015 report released by the Medical Research Council indicates that drinking and driving accounts for up to 53 per cent of annual road deaths in South Africa.[42] Many young people killed in road accidents have blood alcohol concentrations above the legal limit of 0.05g/100ml.

Alternative masculinities

Not all boys, however, succumb to peer pressure to perform seemingly entrenched versions of hegemonic masculinity. Evidence of 'alternative' masculinities – that is, new ways of being a male person, one who is non-violent, non-sexist and non-homophobic – are increasingly being produced.[43] Shefer and colleagues, for example, note in their book From

Boys to Men that there are sub-groups of boys who resist dominant discourses of what it means to be a 'real boy', despite this not being easy to do as it involves being vulnerable to discrimination and subordination. Deevia Bhana found that boys who do not 'fit' hegemonic ideals tend to be subjected to bullying, verbal and physical abuse, exclusion, ridicule and humiliation.

In my study I wanted to test the version of masculinity that encourages and celebrates male dominance and associated risk-taking behaviours, but also try to discover where there might be evidence of resistance or changing attitudes. I also wanted to learn from my young men about some of the psychological strategies they used to resist, subvert and challenge the existing popular norms within their community. I wanted to see how their thinking fitted with the growing body of South African literature claiming new versions of young masculinity that are non-violent, monogamous, modern, responsible and built on respect for self and others, as claimed, for example, in the work of Bhana, Morrell, Ratele and Shefer. What are some of the forces that might effect changes in masculinities, and when and how do such changes occur? What are the psychological processes involved when boys make decisions to identify with one form of masculinity over another or, for that matter, and depending on the context, occupy multiple positions? What kinds of masculine identifications are available to young boys in a South African township?

It is argued that boys who embrace alternative masculinities seek equality, fairness and justice in relationships with others and reject risk-taking behaviours associated with traditional notions of what it means to be a male. The implications and societal benefits could be positive and wide-ranging. Reshma Sathiparsad asserts that developing alternative masculinities may help to address the problem of gender-based violence in South Africa because such boys espouse gender-equitable attitudes and views.[44] Bob Pease found that these boys are also more likely to be actively involved in doing household chores and other activities associated with girls and women.[45]

Despite their progressiveness, alternative voices of masculinity are not popular or publicly celebrated and it is therefore not easy for boys to take on these voices. They are likely to be ridiculed, labelled as 'sissies' and subjected to other forms of bullying. Being a 'different' boy thus comes at a cost, emotionally and psychologically.[46] Boys perform multiple conflicting and contradictory masculinities. How they subvert and defy dominant practices of manhood and masculinity to embrace alternative voices, or merge these multiple, oppositional voices in order to find some kind of balance was especially interesting to me. What strategies to be different do township boys employ?

Morrell found that young black men use different tactics to deal with changing gender relations. Some explicitly resist gender equality and any changes to gender roles; others accommodate these changes in principle but not in practice. Doing household chores and embracing pro-equality views does not mean change in terms of gender politics and transformation, as many boys and men still benefit from the dividends of hegemonic masculinity by mere virtue of the fact that they are males. Notions of hegemonic masculinity thus remain firmly intact and influential, despite the changes that are slowly taking place. Gender change is a highly complex process and occurs within individuals, groups and institutions. It is important to look for signs of gender change, even if, as Lynne Segal observes, they tend to occur in 'slow motion'.[47]

Different people act as role models to boys in the performance of masculinity, including male teachers. In her study into the lives of schoolboys, Pamela Attwell claims that all her participants saw male teachers as strict, less tolerant and less reasonable than female teachers.[48] Morrell notes that 'the model of masculinity presented by the male teachers to students seems unlikely on this reading to generate alternative, more democratic and gentler masculine identities'.[49] It appears that boys have few alternative, positive adult male role models to follow, including also an absence of 'good' fathering, so opportunities for transformation may be lost. In Mamphela Ramphele's *Steering by the Stars: Being Young in South Africa*, young black boys who grew up in New Crossroads in

Cape Town discuss how the pain of absent father figures in their lives impacted on them. Some mention fathers who were cruel, uncaring, unloving and depriving.[50] Ramphele argues that the lack of good male role models influenced some of these young men to become involved in violence and gangs. Other researchers, such as Bhana, Morrell, Ratele and Shefer, argue that the solution to gender-related problems is to find positive voices of masculinity in young boys, which, if nurtured, can be learned and promoted.

Part of the problem or part of the solution?

There is an emerging body of international and national literature pointing to the efficacy of gender-based work with boys and men aimed at positively changing their attitudes and practices around gender and sexuality.[51] In South Africa, the Sonke Gender Justice Network has been working in communities to support boys and men to promote gender equity, prevent domestic and sexual violence, and reduce the spread and impact of HIV and AIDS. This work is aligned with a paradigm shift from what Morrell calls 'old style' feminist theory, in which all boys and men were classed as 'part of the problem in understanding gender relations'.[52] It would be invaluable, in my view, if work on gender studies included studies of adolescent boys in order to challenge traditional ideas about gender oppression and the position of young men, and to contribute to providing a sound theoretical and empirical base to inform intervention programmes. One thing that stood out in my research project and in continuing discussions with the young men who participated in it, is how important it is that these initiatives be started with boys at an early age because 'ideas of what it means to be a man are formed before boys become men'.[53]

Over the years, many 'boys and men studies' have emerged in South Africa, as evidenced in, among others, the work of Bhana, Jewkes, Morrell, Lindegger and Ratele, but one question that might be asked is whether these studies are part of the problem or part of the solution in relation to gender inequalities and difficulties. Catriona Macleod has raised a concern that the proliferation of studies on boys and men might legitimate dominant forms of masculinity in another guise or even undermine the progress that has been made by feminist scholarship.[54] Macleod proposes the possibility of a 'phallocentric trap', arguing that studies on boys and men may inadvertently continue advantaging and privileging men's experiences and voices at the expense of young girls and women by further marginalising them. In response to this concern, Morrell argues that studies on boys and men are not aimed at eradicating feminist scholarship, but rather to add to such scholarship in better understanding men, the social construction of masculinity and gendered relations.[55] Ratele suggests that 'the aim of men's consciousness thought is to give men something along the lines of what women's studies gave to women: self-knowledge. Men's consciousness thought puts men at the centre, just like the women's liberation struggle put women at the forefront.'[56]

The current work on boys and men is aimed at promoting healthy alternative masculinities, gender equality and anti-sexist agendas. So how should the 'new studies on men' relate to feminist scholarship on women? Pease argues that studies on men and women should move in parallel.[57] Feminist and masculinity researchers should work together on issues of feminism and masculinity since they both provide a better understanding of gender relations. However, Pease cautions that women should still be given the space to set their own agendas and projects free from the interferences of men. The idea is that while feminism may serve the interests of men as well as women, researchers also need to explore issues of men and masculinity more critically. By doing so, studies on men will hopefully become part of the solution and not part of the problem. Men and women should sit side by side against the common enemy of problematic versions of hegemonic masculinity.

Understanding masculine subjectivity

It is in the context of such pro-feminist research on boys that my own book is located, with the intention to explore young masculinities within a research tradition that believes it is important to work with boys towards achieving gender equality and progressive masculinities. I have combined social constructionist and psychoanalytic perspectives to understand adolescent boys' subjective construction of their masculinities within a particular social and historical context. Social construction and psychoanalytic theories have been used in combination, both theoretically and methodologically, in many other studies of gender-related issues, for example by Stephen Frosh, Wendy Hollway and Margaret Wetherell. These two approaches are relevant as they highlight how the social and personal aspects of adolescent boys' masculine identity interact.

A theoretical contribution that I hope to make with this book is to the understanding of the feelings, emotional costs and contradictions that occur for boys when negotiating hegemonic and non-hegemonic forms of masculinity. For this reason it is important to use theories that allow for exploration of such masculine subjectivity. There has been a growing interest in exploring the lived or subjective experiences of being and becoming masculine subjects. The notion of subjectivity has been a dominant feature of inquiry in many social science disciplines, including within the field of psychology, as it allows social scientists to engage with more personally experienced or lived aspects of social identity and social location.

Julian Henriques and colleagues' book *Changing the Subject* is regarded as one of the first major texts to grapple with the notion of subjectivity as a focus of academic research in psychology, challenging traditional psychological conceptions that people are mechanically positioned to behave in a particular manner.[58] Wendy Hollway also made a major contribution to the topic in her book *Subjectivity and Method in Psychology*.[59] She refers to subjectivity and the manner in which the term is used as follows: 'individuality and self-awareness – the condition of being a subject is dynamic and multiple, always positioned in relation to discourses and practices'.[60] In this description, Hollway clearly challenges the positivist scientific tradition of viewing the subject as unitary, rational and non-contradictory. She argues that 'it is not that rationality is non-existent, rather that it is always being contested by forces', including the constant struggle to manage repressed material, which includes ideas, feelings, desires and fantasies outside of conscious awareness.[61] Such repressed materials constantly threaten to overwhelm the (masculine) subject. Thus, there are arguably multiple forces governing male subjectivity, including conscious and unconscious contents. This highlights the complexities involved in how adolescent boys deal with subjective experiences of being positioned or positioning themselves as hegemonic or non-hegemonic, and how these positions are negotiated in their daily lives.

The perspective that masculinity is a socially constructed gender category and that gender roles, stereotypes and norms are imposed on the developing boy by parents, teachers and peers, who also subscribe to the same prevailing norms, stereotypes and constructs, has become a dominant theoretical framework in critical gender studies. For example, boys are told at a very young age to avoid anything feminine, such as crying or showing emotions publicly, and are expected to comply with the social constructs of hegemonic masculinity, such as being tough and emotionless. In her seminal text *Gender Trouble*, Judith Butler provides an account of the way in which individuals become gendered and are continually compelled to enact and re-enact gender roles.[62] Men and women constantly *perform* certain gender roles and participate in behaviours required by the cultural norms of masculinity and femininity. This performing entails the 'forced reiterations of norms' within a matrix of constraints.[63] Adolescent boys are often pressurised to indulge in risky behaviours as part of publicly performing the gender role of being male. Those who fail to perform masculine acts are excluded and ostracised. However, Butler claims that some boys may subvert expected norms of masculinity by transgressively engaging in counter-hegemonic gender behaviours. This subverting of gender norms, she asserts, highlights the artificiality of normative constructions of gender. I draw upon Butler's notion of subversion to explore the discursive and behavioural strategies that adolescent boys employ to challenge and reject the dominant norms of hegemonic masculinity. Anthony Elliot explains the notion of performativity as follows: 'Performance involves individuals in continually monitoring the impressions they give off to, and make upon, others. Public identity is thus performed for an audience and the private self knows that such performances are essential to identity and to the maintenance of respect and trust in routine social interaction'.[64] Significantly, this suggests that the self may be split into two, namely a public and a private self. The former is displayed to others and the social world, while the latter is hidden.

Displaying competence to others in the public self is the key signifier of successful masculinity, whereas failure to live up to the public masculine image is anxiety provoking and shameful. It is therefore important continuously to perform the 'correct' male gender role to avoid any stigma or shameful experience. This theoretical framework was useful in helping me to understand the social aspects of masculine identity observable among my study's cohort of adolescent boys. It was not only the social aspects of masculinity in which I was interested; I also wanted to gain insight into the psychological processes of what it means to be a male.

I used a psychoanalytic perspective to identify contradictory desires, conflicts and emotional components within both dominant and subordinated forms of masculinity. This was in line with the aim of contributing theoretically to understanding the emotional costs and tensions that boys experience in negotiating these masculinities. Boys who live alternative versions of masculinity face many challenges, and it is important for researchers to understand what happens psychologically when they negotiate multiple voices of masculinity in their daily lives.

Stephen Frosh supports using psychoanalytic theory as a research tool in gender studies as it offers fertile ground for exploring the problem of what it means to construct a gendered – in this instance a masculine – identity that subverts the categories of gender difference while at the same time employing them.[65] A distinctive characteristic of psychoanalytic theory in relation to gender is its focus on positioning subjective experiences as either masculine or feminine. However, criticisms have been levelled against psychoanalytic theory for its individualising, pathologising and essentialising tendencies and its failure to take context sufficiently into account. Frosh and colleagues argue that 'there is no such thing as "the individual", standing outside the social'.[66]

In the approach I have taken, psychoanalytic theory is not applied in a traditional 'psychotherapeutic' or clinical sense, where the focus is on exchanges between analyst and patient, but is rather located in the tradition of 'applied psychoanalysis' or what Stephen Frosh and Lisa Baraister call 'psychosocial studies', in which the focus is on how the social and the psychodynamic interact.[67] Contemporary applied psychoanalytic theory sees the subject as both social and psychological, with behaviour influenced by the interplay between 'external' social and 'internal' psychical processes. I acknowledge this interplay and recognise that it is important for internal processes to be analysed and interpreted within the context in which the subject is located. I aim to make a theoretical contribution by understanding how adolescent boys subjectively construct their masculinities within a particular social and historical context: in my study the context is a township in post-apartheid South Africa.

It is important to consider the emotional costs of pursuing an appropriate masculine identity. Boys often shift from one position to another in order to manage the expectations of being a 'real man'. Taking up certain subjective positions and letting go of others may evoke feelings of anxiety, loss and sadness. A central question in my study was why adolescent boys invest emotionally in certain subject and subjective positions. What are the conscious or unconscious reasons behind taking up these positions? What are the emotional costs involved in this process? It is arguably only through drawing upon psychoanalytic theory that I am able to explore these kinds of questions. Psychoanalytic theory also provided me with rich language and concepts, such as 'sublimation', 'rationalisation', 'resistance' and 'projection', to interpret some of the psychological processes underpinning the formation of masculinity.

Furthermore, psychoanalytic theory helped me to theorise the male subject's relation to the self, others and society as a whole. As a psychosocial theory, psychoanalysis offered opportunities to explore these intertwined elements by emphasising the ways in which boys mediate their individual lived realities through cultural and social meanings that are in turn overridden with anxieties and desires belonging to the intrapsychic and social realms. In this way, psychoanalysis as a social and critical theory allowed me to move beyond a conceptualisation of male subjectivity as the exclusive effect of either discursive production or of the intrapsychic, but without acknowledging the influence of social factors. Psychoanalysis sees lived experiences and identities as the product of both intrapsychic and social-cultural processes.

In terms of psychoanalytic theory based on the work of Sigmund Freud, fear is at the core of the formation of masculine identity. This fear continues to threaten to engulf the masculine subject, who lives under the continuous threat of a possible psychic disintegration. According to Antony Whitehead, this leads to 'masculine anxiety', which is the fear of collapse in self-identity as a man.[68] This points to the fragile nature of masculinity and goes some way towards explaining why boys and men experience pressure to display their 'manliness' in front of other men, for example, through engaging in risk-taking behaviours – to prove that they are not castrated but are still men. Similarly, Ratele explains that this apparent fearlessness is linked to why men behave violently – to prove that they are not cowards.[69] Failure to live up to the ideal masculine self may produce feelings of insecurity, inadequacy, anxiety and self-doubt about one's sense of manhood. So, in terms of psychoanalytic theory, the masculine subject draws on various defence mechanisms to protect against the possible collapse of the ideal masculine self. This again suggests that masculinity is not stable and coherent as a gender identity but is perhaps constantly experienced as under threat and characterised by internal tensions and contradictions.

Hegemonic or socially sanctioned masculinity represents an ideal image that boys and men aspire to achieve, but the process of achieving it arouses hidden feelings of fear and anxiety. Jacques Lacan sees this struggle to maintain the masculine image as the burden of 'the phallus'.[70]

For Lacan, the phallus is a symbolic representation of potency rather than a purely physical object. In his theory, the phallus is both something that symbolises power and something that is empty. Drawing upon this idea but giving it his own shape, Frosh argues that "'having' the phallus attached to oneself is no guarantee of stability of identity; quite the contrary, it forces the man into an obsession with "getting things straight" and the terror of loss which must seem comic to the penis-free woman. Phallus is such a burden to a man; living up to it becomes the necessary condition of masculinity, which is always in danger of being betrayed and undermined'.[71] The difficulty of sustaining a masculine identity produces an internal struggle for most boys and men. Having the phallus becomes a burden in that it signifies some kind of performance pressure, as per Butler's argument about 'performativity'. Frosh goes further to argue that masculine success is derived from phallic mastery, but this is a complex and multifaceted process, provoking feelings of anxiety and fear about possible failure.

Furthermore, possessing the phallus is such a burden that living up to it becomes implicated in problematic behavioural practices, such as sexual risk-taking, among adolescent boys and young men. The success of today's behaviour as a 'real' man is not sufficient proof for tomorrow. The boy must always do more to prove his masculinity, each act a little riskier. Any failure to sustain a masculine identity produces feelings of inadequacy and a sense that the individual is 'not man enough' or a 'real male'. In this theorisation, boys may continuously find themselves struggling to establish an unchallenged phallus by being willing to demonstrate bravado and avoiding identification with anything feminine. This again suggests that masculinity is a fragile identity that needs constantly to be protected and also defended against threats such as those posed by femininity and homosexuality.

In sum, psychoanalytic theory and its elaboration in the work of critical theorists is a useful framework within which to explore some of the contradictions, fears and anxieties that township boys may experience in negotiating the multiple voices of township masculinity.

3 | Backdrop to Alex – South African Townships and Stories in Context

It is relevant to this study and to other research studies of black youth in South Africa first to have a basic understanding of the role townships have played in the country's political and social history.

Among the many repressive laws of segregation enacted over the years the Group Areas Act of 1950 saw enforced racial separation along lines of colour come into brutal effect. The short- and long-term impact of the uprooting of thousands of families and their relocation into less than hospitable areas, where basic services and amenities were negligible, has been documented in many forms, but the deep disadvantage that came with overcrowded townships and informal settlements was one result.

As the grip of apartheid took hold, many townships in South Africa were the epicentre of the struggle against the oppressive regime. Young and old, people in the townships fought against the regime in a variety of ways: joining liberation movements and organisations and participating in their activities; forming civic organisations; organising protests against local authorities; boycotting municipal services; recruiting young people to go into exile and join the military wings of the different liberation movements; and fighting street battles with the state security forces. Consequently, various other forms of violence also increased in the townships, including violent crimes. This created fear and anxiety, especially with the rise of youth gangs (*bo-tsotsi*), as documented by Clive Glaser in his book *Bo-tsotsi*.[1] Researchers such as Steve Mokwena drew attention to the rise of the 'jackrolling' phenomenon, whereby gang members committed violent crimes that included harassing, kidnapping and raping young women.[2] Some of these incidents led to clashes between comrades and *bo-tsotsi*.[3]

Being a comrade under apartheid meant distinguishing oneself from other members of the community by demonstrating adherence to discipline and respect for community members. Comrades in this context thus saw their role as defenders of 'morality' in the townships, holding to the position that youth leaders needed to behave in a 'disciplined' manner, both when engaged as members of organisations and as members of the community.[4] Comrades were thus accorded the responsibility of punishing suspected criminals (*tsotsis*), gang members, informers/spies or ill-disciplined members of their organisations.[5] Some punishments involved 'necklacing' – putting a tyre around a person's neck, pouring petrol on it and setting the person alight.

Undoubtedly, the apartheid regime influenced young male township comrades and activists to develop certain notions of a militarised/struggle masculinity, which was perceived as positive.[6] As part of constructing this form of masculinity, these young men were expected to be strong, brave, tough, fearless, aggressive and violent. Many were heavily influenced to incorporate these qualities into a militarised kind of masculine identity that went hand in hand with their active involvement in politics and violent protest activities aimed at defeating the apartheid regime.[7] Numerous young men (and women) were arrested, tortured and killed, primarily by state security forces, as a consequence of joining the liberation struggle.[8]

The focus of an earlier research project in which I was involved was about understanding the experiences of young men who were involved in the anti-apartheid struggle in the townships of Katlehong, Thokoza and Vosloorus in Gauteng province. The key informants in that study spoke about the violence that took place between members/supporters of the African National Congress (ANC)- and the Inkatha Freedom Party (IFP)-aligned self-defence units (SDUs). The participants in that study had asserted in the interviews that young men needed to prove during this violence (what some termed 'black-on-black violence') that they were brave, tough and fearless in the face of the enemy. Certain notions of militarised masculinities developed during that period and some young men after 1994 were still struggling to deal with the intractability of these identities and function optimally in the new democratic dispensation.[9]

Tsotsi masculinity, in contrast, was a negatively defined masculinity, associated with anti-social behaviour. *Tsotsis* nevertheless held a powerful identity since they were feared for their potential to be extremely violent. Although the distinctions between comrade and *tsotsi* identity were not always clear-cut, there was a period in which there was serious conflict between such groups in the townships, particularly in the 1980s and early 1990s. However, both identities represented ways of accruing power as young black men at that time.

It is important that the political history inherent in South African townships be kept in mind and that township masculinities are understood as a product of a particular system and as emerging out of a particular context.

*

Townships as living spaces have not remained static since the transition to a democratic government in 1994. Many have grown in terms of population size and are still characterised by a lack of access to basic services such as housing, clean running water, and working drainage and sewerage systems. These are the poor living conditions in which many black people live.

For adolescent boys growing up in a township today, the relevance of the political history, as well as the deprived circumstances that largely prevail to greater or less degrees, informed the questions as a researcher that I would ask. What kinds of young adults would these boys become? Would their identities as young black men be shaped by their living circumstances in a township? How would this environment influence their masculine identities? Would it influence their identities positively or negatively? Is there any hope for young black men growing up in these spaces or is their future one of doom and gloom? Who supports young black men in negotiating their masculine identities in these township spaces? What kind of support can be given to them or is it a question of 'black man, you are on your own', as Steve Bantu Biko, the leader of the Black Consciousness movement, asserted in the 1970s?

The township of Alexandra served as a good research area to conduct this study for a number of reasons. Alex is a predominantly black township situated 13 kilometres from the centre of Johannesburg, in the north-eastern suburbs. Poverty levels in Alex are reported to be high, especially when contrasted with the wealth of the neighbouring suburb of Sandton, just 4 kilometres away. Alex was established in 1912 to provide a base for a black labour pool to serve the white population in the northern suburbs of Johannesburg. The majority of people in Alex came to Johannesburg from rural areas in search of work.[10]

Today, Alexandra, like many other townships, faces a myriad social and environmental problems, such as poverty, high unemployment, overcrowding, crime, pollution, poor electricity supply, lack of clean water, substance abuse, child neglect and women abuse. Due to the dire circumstances in which most residents live, and the area's close proximity to wealthy suburbs, crime committed by young men is high, with the rationale being that this is a way they can survive adversity.

There is also a shortage of housing in Alex, which has resulted in overcrowding and many people living in shacks. Given the lack of proper drainage, uncollected refuse and people living very close to one another, residents are predisposed to health problems and vulnerable to infectious diseases. In terms of healthcare, those who earn more tend to seek private-sector healthcare outside of Alex, while poorer households for the most part utilise public healthcare facilities.

While Alex has particular unique features, many young men in other South African townships grow up in similar circumstances to those described above. These youths, the future adults in society, form a significant proportion of the South African population. It is thus important to study the experiences of these young men growing up in adverse environments with non-optimal life circumstances, conditions that are not atypical for youth in a range of global contexts. Such young men may be particularly at risk of experiencing problematic identity-development trajectories.

There is much rich material for social inquiry and research to be uncovered in a township environment, but my focus was on gender identity and different expressions of masculinity, and, importantly, on filling the gap I had identified in our understanding of how boys construct their masculinity – hence my question 'what makes a man a man?' Raewyn Connell argues that masculinity is not a single construct or phenomenon, but differs in expression from one context to another.[11] The decision to 'choose' or 'live' one form of masculinity over any other is influenced by factors such as culture, race, class and ethnicity. I wanted to explore the multiple voices of masculinity among young township men at this point in time and in a particular setting. The expression of masculinity in contemporary South Africa is also influenced by the changed political landscape and the emergence of alternative, competing gender identities, which in some respects challenge the dominant norms of hegemonic masculinity. As masculinities are increasingly subjected to interrogation, both globally and nationally, adolescent boys and young men are likely to experience contradictions in negotiating their way around them.

A further reason for choosing a township context as the focus area of this study was to explore how township boys position themselves in relation to hegemonic practices of masculinity in the 'new' South Africa. Constructions of masculinity change over time. Glaser's study, for example, revealed that *tsotsi* masculinity was very popular in South African black townships, including Alex, during the apartheid years.[12] As noted earlier, the youth in Alex were also at the forefront of the struggle against apartheid and participated in paramilitary activities (see, for example, Phil Bonner and Noor Nieftagodien for a detailed history of Alex and its role in struggle politics).[13] By focusing on the experiences of contemporary youth in Alex, I was keen to investigate how the construction of masculine identities has changed after 1994, with a specific focus on adolescent boys and their journey to adulthood.

Getting the picture

The adolescent boys who were to become my focus group were recruited in 2007 from three high schools in Alexandra. They ranged between the ages of 13 and 18 and were in grades 10, 11 and 12. Because the school principals were responsible for authorising the study in their schools, I held meetings with each of them to explain the nature of the study, including getting permission from parents as the boys were minors at the time. I also got permission from the provincial Department of Education to conduct the study.

In the meetings, I explained that I wanted to conduct research into what it entails to be a boy in Alex. I also explained what participation in the study would involve. All the adolescent boys who expressed an interest in taking part in the study were given forms to take home for their parents to read and sign, and the parental consent forms were returned to me. Ultimately, 32 adolescent boys were recruited, exceeding the 18 that I had initially wanted, since there was considerable interest in participating in the study. I decided that the larger sample would allow for richer and deeper data.

At the beginning of the study, the boys selected were given disposable cameras and asked to take 27 photos (the total number available on the film) under the theme 'My life as a young black man in the new South Africa'. In taking their photos, they were encouraged to think about the following questions: What is it like to be a boy? What are the things that make boys feel like 'real' boys? How do boys spend their time? What are some of the challenges boys face? What do other people (for example, friends, parents, teachers and girlfriends) expect from boys? What makes some boys more popular than others? Are there alternative ways of being a boy? Do you ever imagine being different to other boys?

With the central theme and the prompting questions in mind, the boys were given a period of two weeks to take their photographs. This gave them the space and time to think about how they wanted to represent themselves, but it also required them to focus on the task. After two weeks, I arranged to collect all the disposable cameras. As agreed to by the boys, two sets of the photographs were processed – one set was placed in an album (entitled 'My life as a young black man') and returned to the boy who had taken them, and I retained the duplicate set.

A total of 776 photos were taken. All of them were used to facilitate semi-structured individual interviews in which the boys' life stories were shared. In the interviews, they were asked to describe each photograph they had taken and to explain why and how they had decided to capture that particular image. What was the intention in taking a particular photo and what were the thoughts, fantasies, feelings and emotions that accompanied it, both at the time of taking it and in the interview? (Figures 1-6 are some of the early photos.)[14]

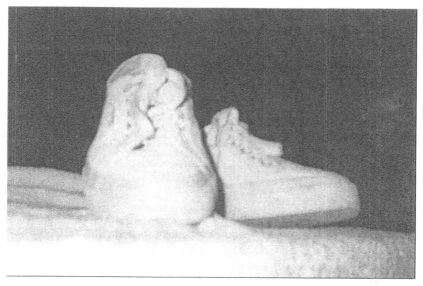

Figure 1: Superga shoes, which were described as popular among boys in Alexandra township.

Figure 2: ABSA Bank. Many boys spoke about the need to have money and how access to money also facilitated their access to girls and brand-name clothes.

Figure 3: Movies that boys watch, including pornographic movies which, the boys explained, were easy to access on their cell phones as well.

Figure 4: Many boys spoke about their fantasies of owning fancy cars. They also complained bitterly about older men who drive these flashy cars and date young girls.

Figure 5: All the boys spoke about fantasies of owning big houses in the future as opposed to living in shacks in Alex.

Figure 6: Some boys spoke about the importance of being involved in household chores such as cooking and cleaning.

Using photographs as a route in to discussing masculinity seemed to produce a heightened level of engagement on the part of the boys – 'I really enjoyed taking nice photos about being a boy' – and they found the project interesting. Both the content of the images as well as the boys' elaborations about them provided useful data. In describing their photos, the boys were the authors of their own narratives and were able to tell their stories spontaneously without feeling pressurised about what views might be wrong or right. Through their photos and descriptions, they shared their everyday lived experiences of what it meant to be a boy as well as their fantasies about life and their future expectations as young males. Some of these included owning expensive cars and big houses with swimming pools. It was clear that they had put considerable thought and effort into deciding which photos to take and what those photos represented in their daily lives – and they also enjoyed explaining the context within which some of the photos were taken.

Many boys commented that the individual interviews, which were conducted after school hours or over the weekend, were valuable to them ('Talking "man to man" is what I needed,' one of them told me) as the researcher was a male. In the interviews, I asked them to describe each photograph they had taken and say why they had decided to take it, and I gave them the space and the time to do this. As a result a lot of the interviews were fairly long as each photo and the narrative associated with it was covered. Each interview took more than an hour, and in some cases two to three hours.

Individual and group interviews

In general the boys seemed more relaxed and open in the individual interviews than they did in the focus groups. The individual interviews also allowed me to identify any difficulties that the young men faced in negotiating the multiple voices of masculinity. There were many contradictions in their narratives, which appeared to reflect the complexity of being a young black man engaging with the diverse aspects of establishing a gender identity.

I was both flexible and reflexive. For instance, where relevant, I commented on the boys' non-verbal cues to elicit more information (for example, 'It seems you were quite uncomfortable when I asked about your religious beliefs. Can you tell me what that is about?' 'It seems you were bit emotional when you spoke about not knowing your father?'). Commenting on the boys' non-verbal cues proved to be enriching. The boys were able to express their hurt feelings, emotions, fears and anxieties connected to particular issues. In the individual interviews, over time I ensured that a wide range of issues were covered, such as their self-definition as male/masculine; role models; their relationships with other boys and with girls; intimacy and friendships; sexual practices; violence; career aspirations; and substance abuse. I explored the difficulties that the boys encountered in their daily lives and how these also related to other social structures. Although the style of the interviews was non-directive, I challenged the boys to reflect on the inconsistencies and contradictions in their narratives so that they could freely talk about their uncertainties over friendships, disappointment with parents, anger with absent or unavailable fathers, feelings of rejection by girls, fears of being seen as gay, feelings about suicide, and aspirations for the future, among other issues. Many boys reflected that the individual interviews were their first experiences of meeting someone who asked them such personal questions in a non-judgemental way, which made them think about who they were, their wishes and aspirations in life and some of the difficulties they encountered daily. Some boys became very emotional in the interviews, especially when they spoke about their absent fathers and the pain that this caused in their lives.

Following the individual interviews, I invited each boy to a group interview, with five to six boys per group. All the group meetings were held at school after school hours. For group meetings, each boy was asked to choose 5 of his 27 images that best described him and to share them with the other boys in the group. I was interested to see whether the photo-narratives that the boys shared in individual interviews remained consistent when articulated in a focus group with other boys or whether they changed, possibly because of feeling pressurised to comply with the dominant norms of hegemonic masculinity.

While some boys were initially embarrassed to show their photos in the group, for others the group interview process became something of a game as they competed with each other to give the most comprehensive information about their images. Some were curious about what the other boys' photos meant or represented. No one, however, wanted to be the first person to share his photos, so I asked the boys to take turns to share one photo at a time. Interestingly, the first photos they shared were of material things such as cars, cell phones and fashionable items like brand-name shoes and clothing. Photos that included mothers, or that showed boys doing things that were considered unmanly, such as cooking and cleaning, were never shared in the group interviews.

For me this raised a number of questions. What did it say about the boys that only photos that were considered masculine were shared in the group interview? Why did they not share certain photos that included their personal stories? What was their fear or anxiety around sharing photos that were personal or considered unmanly? Did this confirm that being a 'real' boy was heavily sanctioned by other boys – that they were not free to be who they were because they always needed to rely on other boys for affirmation and confirmation?

What, more broadly, did this say about boyhood?

Using individual and focus group interviews provided me with rich information, insights and ideas about what it means to be a boy. I was also able to observe how the boys 'policed' and 'regulated' one another. Interestingly, I noted that some boys changed the stories they had shared about certain photos with me in their one-on-one interview when it came to talking about them in a focus group setting. For example, when discussing photos of girls in the individual interviews, some boys voiced the view that it was important for boys to have only one partner. However, this view changed in the group sessions, where they supported other boys' views that a 'boy cannot have only one girlfriend'. All the boys took turns to assert in the group interviews that having more than one girlfriend was a good thing ('it is part of male nature for boys to have many girlfriends because you have two hands, you have two ears, two eyes – why then must you have one girlfriend?') For them, it was normal behaviour for a boy to have more than one girlfriend, and inconceivable that I even asked the question. This view was shared by all the boys without any interrogation, including those who had expressed a different opinion in the individual interviews.

Why did these boys not object and assert the view they had shared with me in the individual interviews? Was their fear and anxiety around raising non-normative views or were they simply performing their expected gender roles? What would have happened if they had raised their differing opinions? Would they have been ridiculed or called derogatory names? Did this mean that it is compulsory for all boys to comply with certain practices of boyhood, even though these practices might be sexist or homophobic?

A further observation was that the boys shared intense personal feelings in the individual interviews but not in the group meetings. Did this imply that boys do not share their emotions with one another? How does lack of emotional expression affect boys' relationships with other boys? If hegemonic masculinity frowns on males expressing 'sissy stuff' when it comes to emotions, does this suggest that the only feelings they can legitimately show are anger and aggression? How does the 'no sissy stuff' mantra affect boys' lives?

After all the interviews had been transcribed, I decided to conduct follow-up individual interviews with 20 of the boys. Ten showed strong conformity to hegemonic ideals and ten seemed to subscribe to apparently alternative versions of masculinity. This is not to say the distinction was clear because masculine identities are non-static and change continuously. Some boys occupied multiple positions of what it meant to be a township boy, vacillating between hegemonic and alternative voices, while others were rigid in their positions. My intention with these follow-up individual interviews, which were conducted two to three months after the initial ones, was to better explore hegemonic and counter-hegemonic masculinities. I was fairly specific about pursuing the major themes I had discerned in the transcripts, but I also wanted to clarify and explore contradictions and gaps I had identified in their first-interview material.

About a week before the second interview I gave each of the boys the transcript of his first one to read and think about. When we met I first asked each boy whether the transcript accurately reflected what he had said in that first private interview with me and them I asked him for his thoughts about the material or the things he had said. Was there anything that he wanted to add or change, for example, or had anything changed markedly since then? I also asked the boys to elaborate on interesting points and issues.

I found the second interviews very useful in clarifying issues, and for supplementing narratives that had emerged in both the earlier individual interviews and the focus groups. The boys told me they found the follow-up individual interviews useful, too, in helping them to reflect at a deeper level on what it meant for them to be boys in their township context. 'I wish these meetings can continue for ever and ever,' one of them confided.

*

As these Alex adolescents got to know and trust me and grew older and became young men, they openly shared their deep feelings and emotions with me about the tensions, contradictions and challenges of being young black men in a township. Later interviews focused on specific issues such as relationships with steady partners, being fathers, searching for job opportunities, entering the world of work, being retrenched, dealing with issues of race and racism, and paying *lobola* and getting married.

Follow-up interviews with the participants allowed them to talk about almost everything in their personal lives. Many of these personal stories were shared freely because over the years we had established a close rapport. They often took the lead in arranging interview sessions. All of them noted that the interviews served as an opportunity for them to reflect on their identities as young men, most of whom had grown up without fathers or father figures to talk to about their daily challenges. I tape-recorded and transcribed each session for further data analysis.

My decision to undertake a longitudinal study bore rich fruit. Regular contact over years and the consistency of the individual interview style of communication allowed me to observe and note major changes in the boys' personal lives and learn of the challenges they encountered in their transition from adolescence to young adulthood. I got to see boys without father figures in their lives become fathers themselves and to understand their feelings about this. I learned from them about their lived experience of violent behaviours as adolescent boys in schools, about their relationships with girls and girlfriends, and the mothers of their children, about both coming out as gay and dealing with homophobia, and about finding employment in a difficult economy and the opportunities and frustrations in trying to build careers.

Much of the data that I was able to record and subsequently analyse and share, both in defending it as my doctoral thesis and later in the form of this book, would not have emerged if I had not followed these participants over a period of close on 12 years, thereby demonstrating the value of a longitudinal study.

4 | Absent Fathers, Present Mothers

The picture that emerged from my Alexandra-based group of young men was that a clear majority lived with little or no direct contact with their fathers. A few lived with older male figures in their homes such as grandparents, brothers and uncles – men who could be regarded as 'social fathers' – but most had, at best, intermittent contact with their biological fathers. Of the 32 participants I started off with in this study, 19 had no contact with their fathers or did not know the identity of their fathers; 7 knew their fathers but they had separated from their mothers; 4 were living with their fathers but described them as emotionally absent; and 2 had lost their fathers through death.

This small sample from one South African township has resonance with a report in 2018 on the state of fatherhood in the country as a whole, which revealed that a majority of children grow up without father figures in their lives.[1] The report is comprehensive and discusses various causes and dynamics of father absence in South Africa and its associated consequences.

Primary themes from the interviews and focus group discussions I had with the young men included: dealing with the absence of a father figure; fantasies around meeting the absent father; the agency of mothers in dealing with the absent father; and ideals around future fathering. In this chapter, 'father absence' refers to fathers who are absent through death, absent with occasional contact, absent with regular contact and absent with no contact at all.[2]

It is important here, again, to take the context of Alexandra township into account when discussing the participants' narratives. The majority of families in Alex live in shacks, many of which are not big enough to accommodate all members of the household. As a result, many families are dispersed and family members do not necessarily live under the same roof. For example, some of the boys told me that they did not live in the same shack with their brothers, who instead were renting their own backyard shacks, and they seldom saw them. Uncles or grandparents were either around in other parts of Alex or back at home in the rural areas or other townships in South Africa. It was rare in the whole sample to find participants living with other male figures such as uncles or grandparents in this township context.

Consequently, many participants felt there were no available male role models to guide them in terms of what it meant to be a boy. Only five boys were living with both their father and mother at the time of the initial interviews. However, ready access to their fathers did not automatically translate into these relationships being perceived in a positive light. Some boys described their fathers as being emotionally abusive, which created an emotional distance between them and made it difficult for them to talk to their fathers. Kgosi,[3] one of the youngest boys in the study when I met him, was one who grew up without his father – his father had been forced to take a paternity test when Kgosi's mother was pregnant with him. This made Kgosi feel rejected by his biological father. He did not thrive academically at school and could often be found at the school toilets playing dice with his friends. He was close to his mother, however, and when she died before he finished school, Kgosi took it very hard.

I found it significant during the photo-taking part of the project that although many of the boys took photos of cars, clothes, cell phones, girls and friends during the study, none had photos of fathers or older male figures in their lives. Consciously or unconsciously, this may have revealed the living world of these young men characterised by the absence of male figures in their personal lives. Individual interviews were useful in allowing the boys the space to talk about their disappointment with absent fathers. Many spoke about this issue at length, without much probing from my side. They talked about the difficulty of not knowing their fathers, describing this as very painful and, when they were adolescents at school, a reason they avoided talking about the subject. All 19 of the boys who told me that they did not know their fathers had never shared this information with their male peers or teachers – they either avoided the topic altogether or remained silent when their friends talked about their dads. They were envious of friends who knew their fathers and experienced it as painful to hear them talk about their relationships with them. Many of the boys said they were ashamed and embarrassed to tell their male friends that they did not know their fathers. This was considered a sensitive and private matter because it raised personal questions about their identity.

Themba, short and stocky and a talented soccer player, who focused more on his formidable ball skills than on his homework, did not know who his father was and this affected his sense of identity: 'It is very embarrassing to tell your friends that you do not know your father and that you do not know who you are.' For Themba, talking to his peers about his absent father evoked feelings of shame about being an 'illegitimate' as opposed to 'legitimate' child who knew his biological father. 'You feel maybe you were born by mistake,' he said. Consequently, and because of the humiliation he attached to his status of not knowing his father, he tended to avoid conversations about fathers. On the occasions when he did talk about his absent father he became highly emotional. There was a wistfulness in his voice when he said: 'I really wish my father was staying with us. I miss him ...'.

Many of the boys were very emotional when they spoke about their absent fathers in the interviews and many also seemed angry at their fathers for not having played any positive role in their lives.

Fifteen-year-old Thabiso was less reticent about talking about his absent father, who lived elsewhere with another woman and her children (something he resented) but still I could see it was difficult for him to discuss the issue. He had had no contact with his father since 2003 and he confessed to being ashamed to tell his teachers the truth about why his father did not attend parents' meetings. He did not want them to know that he had no contact with his father. His solution – 'I had no choice' – was to fabricate a story that allowed him to save face: he told his teachers that his father worked at night. Thabiso was not shy about his situation, though; talking openly about it, he said, helped him cope.

It must be remembered that when I first interviewed these boys they were adolescents, one as young as 13. This is a period of development during which many young boys ask identity-related questions: Who am I? Who is my father? Why did he leave? Where is he? What does he look like? Am I like my father at all? Some of the boys experienced a form of 'identity crisis' in relation to not knowing their fathers, but it seemed they never shared these feelings of frustration and suffering with their friends. It is possible that adolescent boys avoid talking to their male peers about absent father figures because the topic is likely to evoke sad feelings, and these are emotions that boys feel they need to avoid expressing in 'public' spaces. Boys who publicly express such feelings and emotions are seen as 'sissies' and their sense of manhood is questioned.[4]

In the interviews, some participants talked about their envy of boys who had access to caring and loving fathers, although considerable emphasis was also placed on the role that these fathers played in offering material provision. They wished their fathers were also available to provide financial resources so that they could, for example, buy expensive brand-name clothes to impress or fit in with their peers. The boys seemed to draw on the traditional or conventional notion that fathers should be breadwinners and provide material resources for their children. This reduction of fathers to being bank ATMs suggests that the boys perceived a father's role to be that of an economic provider rather than someone who meets the emotional needs of his children.[5] 'Good' fathering is thereby reduced to a man's ability to meet the material needs of his children. This view results in unemployed fathers feeling that they are not 'good enough' due to their inability to financially support their children.[6]

Making contact with their fathers seemed to preoccupy many of the boys who did not know their fathers and this desire to meet them was a constant refrain in our conversations. However, some boys recognised that such meetings might be complicated and evoke conflicting feelings and emotions.

Simon, who was one of the most intelligent and articulate of the participants, and who often took the role of teacher in our group discussions, had a clear sense of self from the beginning. He was a tall boy, always neat and tidy, who carried himself with confidence. He had three brothers he looked up to who, in a sense, were father figures to him in the absence of his own father. Simon, too, felt a desire to meet his father, but he was cautious. 'I do not want to have that tight relationship with him,' he explained, 'but I would like to meet him. By any chance if he comes back it is not like I am going to hate him or anything. I would forgive him, simple! But then it would not be like the same. It's not going to be like back to normal, happily ever after. No, it can't be like that because he wasn't there.'

Most of the boys were noticeably emotional when they spoke about their absent fathers. They were also conflicted about how they would react if their fathers returned, given their anger at their fathers for not having been there when they were growing up. However, all the boys concluded that they would forgive their fathers in order to heal emotionally, even though this would not be easy. Forgiveness seemed to signify letting go of suppressed feelings of anger and disappointment at their absent fathers.

Some boys knew where their fathers lived and although their fathers also knew where they lived, they made no effort to contact them as their sons. The boys knew that their fathers were living with other women and their children and felt angry not only with their fathers but also with their female partners for having taken away their fathers to support their own children, without any support for them. With Thabiso, this was an especially sore point, and he felt very neglected by his father. However, he said he had no option but to live with it and had accepted the situation. Rejection by their fathers was a strong thread running through these conversations and it obviously cut deeply.

Nathan was in Grade 10 when I met him. He had a warm and calm personality and a pleasant manner. He was the last-born in his family and very close to his mother. His father, he said, treated his mother very badly, which made him sad and angry. His father now lived in Tembisa, a township close by, with another woman and did not keep in touch with his son in Alex, although Nathan has made many attempts to call him and talk to him. The last time he saw his father was in 2002. 'I miss him,' Nathan said simply. 'When I call, he turns off the phone.' Despite what his father had put him through, he was not deterred from wanting to get married one day and have a family. He would 'do right', he said, by his kids.

Some of the boys spoke about their feelings of depression due to the lack of a father figure in their lives and some cried openly in the individual interviews.

William was one who struggled with depression and, at 16, the age he was when we started on the research project, he already exuded a general feeling of hopelessness. He was not optimistic about the future and had no personal goals or even dreams to share; nor was he interested in his schoolwork. He had brothers but, unlike Simon, he did not have any relationship with them. On occasion he spoke about feeling suicidal. He was 10 when his father left, and he still did not know the reason for his departure. The gap his father's absence left in his internal world was a significant one and when he talked about his father his pain was all too obvious.

I can say because he [his father] was supposed to have been around at that time and play a father figure; and show me what being a guy means, and how was I supposed to carry myself. So he was never there and I had to see stuff for myself. Eish! I feel empty in a way.

Like there is a space that is left opened. Eish! No one! I had to see things for myself. I started doing bad things at an early stage like smoking, drinking and going to parties. And I know if my father was here, I wouldn't have done that. So I got freedom at an early age. And as you can understand, in the township life is fast, things happen. You feel sad and there are moments where one wishes he was dead.

He contended that his lack of access to a father had influenced him to behave recklessly and to start smoking and drinking at a young age. It has to be asked, of course, whether William was perhaps using his home background as an excuse for his risk-taking behaviours, since other boys in the study who also had no father figures did not necessarily engage in such behaviours. That said, some of these boys did have other male figures to help them with positive older male identifications. In his narrative, William mentioned that he did not have anyone to act as his male role model. Arguably, good fathering (from either a biological father or any substitute male figure) enables a boy child to reconcile opposing elements in his psyche.[7] William, however, did not have any 'good' internal paternal figure to regulate his internal world and fill the 'empty space' left by his absent father. He did have two older brothers, but rarely talked to them. They were not positive role models, he said, because they also drank and smoked heavily. 'Everyone was minding his own business' after his father left, he said. The subsequent sense of 'emptiness' and the lack of alternative male role models left him vulnerable to peer pressure to indulge in risk-taking activities. He was remorseful about engaging in such behaviours, however. He even went so far as to suggest not only that he wished his father was around to play a positive father figure role, but also to discipline him. He seemed to be seeking a male to take an active interest in and set boundaries for him. Despite some insight into his own self-destructiveness, he felt unable to change his behaviour without some external structure and validation.

William's response to his father's abandonment of his family left me with the sense that William had less hope, less investment in the future and therefore less motivation to change. As a result, he behaved recklessly. Later, William started reflecting differently on his behaviour as a young black man and the sense he made of his life growing up without a father.

Benny was a boy who had never met his father. He was not doing well in school and volunteered that he some behavioural problems, such as drinking and smoking. He was tall and skinny and his school shoes were always buffed so that they shone. In our second, follow-up interview, he told me that our initial discussion had evoked feelings in him about his absent father and his own sense of identity – 'I want to know who I am,' he said. 'I want to know who my father is.' After the first interview he had gone home and asked his mother about his father. His mother told him that his father had left while she was still pregnant and that she had lost contact with him. However, she had heard he was living in a remote rural area in Limpopo province. Benny wanted to know what his father looked like. 'Does he look like me?' he asked rhetorically in the interview. It was interesting to observe how Benny drew on a cultural discourse to explain his risk-taking behaviours as an adolescent. He said that he wanted to change his surname to his father's surname because he saw this as important for acceptance by his father's ancestors. Furthermore, he added that he wanted to adopt his father's culture so as to align with his line of heritage. Benny attributed some of his behavioural problems, the smoking, drinking and poor academic performance, to a lack of connection with his father's ancestors. He believed the only solution to his problems was to meet his father and perform certain rituals to cleanse himself so that he could start behaving like a 'real' man.

All the boys regarded fathers as important male figures who had to help their sons to develop certain attributes of masculinity. Such identification with these male figures in the community was a crucial marker of being a 'real' boy. Benny wanted to identify with his father by taking his surname, recognising that this would hold some symbolic meaning for him. Unfortunately, he did not succeed in tracing and locating his father. He asserted that, like the other boys whose situations were similar to his, he was frustrated that he had never met his father and shared the fantasy that his father would have helped him to better understand what it meant to be an adolescent boy and to become a man by giving him guidance and support.

However, some boys (Lesley and Tato were two) were disappointed after meeting their fathers as they discovered that their 'fantasised fathers' were not the same as the fathers they met. They struggled to form any emotional bond with them. Lesley felt his father was aloof and distant. Tato shared the same feelings, but mentioned that he was also conflicted about whether to forgive his father or not for having been absent in his life.

In their research published in 2014 Motlalepule Nathane-Taulela and Mzikazi Nduna found that discovering fathers did not resolve their participants' feelings, especially if both parties fail to connect and reconnect emotionally.[8] They concluded that forming positive relationship depends on the child and father's common interest in dealing with feelings and emotions associated with their new relationship.

*

Dealing with the absence of a deceased father was a major challenge faced by two of the boys in the study.

In his individual interview, 17-year-old Xander spoke at length about his father, who had died when he was 4 years old. This loss was later followed by the death of his mother when he was in Grade 10. Xander told me that his mother's death had evoked unresolved issues about his father's death:

> When I was 12 years old I realised that I did not have a father, then I started questioning and finding that my questions are being ignored. Those questions were being ignored until my mother died. So I remained clueless. I do not even know the picture of my father. I had a stepfather, but it was just not good enough. It was not good enough for me because I needed a father who cares about me, because I am his organism. So if it's a stepfather, he does not really care.

Talking about the loss of his parents evoked strong emotions in him and at times he became tearful. He was frustrated that he had no memory of his father and not even his 'picture' to relate to as part of the memory process. Xander seemed angry that his questions about his father had been ignored and, now that his mother had also died, he remained 'clueless'. He repeatedly stated that he wished his father was still alive or that he at least had some photographs of him. It was difficult, he said, for him to mourn or identify with a father figure whom he could not remember or even visualise. Like many of the other boys in the study, Xander confirmed that growing up without knowing his father was not easy. It was also painful for him to hear his friends at school talking about their fathers and he felt he had 'nothing' to share. Xander did not say much about his stepfather, but it seemed he was not very close to him. He said that he had never had a positive male figure to identify with, except his uncle, who lived somewhere in KwaZulu-Natal and with whom he had lost contact. Xander appeared to be coping with his mother's death, however, despite all the emotions shared:

> I am coping, I am trying to forget about it, live with it, appreciate that; except that they are gone now, and they will never come back. I am deciding to be a role model to other people now. I am deciding that my little siblings must look up to me when they are in problems and in pain and I will be there for them. After all, you do not need to hide your feelings because if you hide them they kill you. They're just in there inside you wanting to go out. And if they do not get a space to go out you end up collapsing. This pain is in there and you do not want to take it out. So it's better if you cry it all out.

Xander was quite a popular boy at school, got on well with his teachers and was a peer counseller. He was involved in conducting a number of workshops, something he seemed to enjoy, and was confident in giving feedback on these at school assemblies. Despite the misfortune in his own life, particularly the recent loss of his mother who, he said, had been central to his life, he showed a great deal of compassion towards others. He even started a project at school encouraging fellow students to donate clothes to give to those less fortunate than themselves.

Clearly, Xander felt obliged to take on the adult male role of looking after his younger siblings following his parents' deaths, thus becoming 'parentified'. This parentification had a considerable impact on him as he did not have the opportunity to be a boy child and felt pressurised to be responsible and strong for his younger siblings, as well as a role model for other people. He felt that there were no positive male role models in Alex, including male teachers at his school, adding, 'It is wrong for teachers to date schoolgirls and give them marks. It is wrong because they need to be role models to us young boys.'

Interestingly, Xander himself assumed the role of a responsible male figure at school and was actively involved in the Learners' Representative Council. In his capacity as a male peer counsellor, he aimed to help his peers deal with their personal problems. He was living with an aunt who, he said, took good care of him and treated him as her own, and all in all he appeared to be coping well with his parents' deaths.

The question to be asked is, are father or male figures a core or necessary part of masculine development? Xander and some of the other boys were able to construct positive male identities that were not risk taking, despite the lack of father figures in their lives and possibly even in reaction to this absence, by creating positive role models for other boys. Xander attributed his positive sense of self to his aunt, who had been very supportive since his mother's death. He told me he saw his aunt as one of his role models.

*

The boys might not have had photos of their fathers, but some did have photos of their mothers. They felt their mothers had played a significant role in shaping their positive characters, despite the absence of father figures in their lives. They described their mothers as positive, dependable role models. 'I would not be who I am,' Simon asserted, 'if it was not [for] my mother. I can say she is my hero.' He described his mother as a hardworking person who managed to support all her children on her own.

The boys' celebration of mothers as positive role models is contrary to the existing literature, which tends to present single motherhood as a source of emotional problems for many adolescent boys. It was clear in all the stories they shared with me that these boys felt their mothers provided adequate or good support in the absence of their fathers. Many boys described their mothers as 'symbolically' filling the void left by absent father figures, supporting the psychoanalytic writer Jacques Lacan's view that the mother can symbolically play the role of the father in his absence in order to encourage a healthy sense of self in the boy child.[9]

Some boys also spoke about how their mothers were open to talking to them about sex, HIV and AIDS and condom use. Those boys who lived with both their parents reported that it was difficult to talk to their fathers about these topics. Many boys described their mothers as warm and approachable while fathers were mostly described as too strict, aloof and distant. Furthermore, the boys did not trust their fathers enough to talk to them about emotional problems out of a fear of being seen as weak or unmanly. Conversely, they experienced their mothers as containing and empathetic in responding to their feelings and emotions. The boys appreciated and valued that their mothers affirmed their sense of masculinity and allowed them to talk about their feelings, fears and anxieties without making them feel they were not 'man enough'. Most boys felt that their mothers seemingly gave them a sense of security in helping them deal with the anxieties of what it meant to be an adolescent boy in the absence of father figures, with a lot reassurance that it was fine for them to talk openly about their feelings.

One can therefore argue that mothers played a significant role in helping their sons negotiate the multiple voices of masculinity. On the whole, it appears that mothers were attuned to meeting the emotional needs of their adolescent sons in a way that made them feel safe and emotionally connected to their mothers. Thus, it cannot be simplistically assumed that the absence of a father will necessarily result in a maladjusted boy child. Some mothers appear to have the capacity to help their sons develop a secure masculine gender identity.

5 | Pressures to Perform – *Tsotsi* Boys vs Academic Achievement

In keeping with several other South African studies, the boys in this study also characterised themselves and their peers according to self-generated and commonly understood typologies, reflecting that adolescent identities within their community are not homogeneous.[1] All the participants mentioned that boys are not the same and that there are different 'types' of boys at school: *tsotsi* boys (naughty/violent boys), academic boys, *sex-jaro* boys (popular with girls), Christian boys, *cheese* boys (rich boys) and gay boys. Most boys do not fit neatly into one category, however. Adolescent boys often vacillate between and identify with multiple positions, confirming Stephen Frosh and colleagues' view that masculinities are fluid, multiple and often contradictory.[2]

Some interesting complexities were revealed during my interviews with the adolescent boys in Alexandra township in relation to how boys simultaneously accept and reject certain masculine practices in their daily lives, depending on the contexts in which they find themselves.

Tsotsi boys were described as boys who miss classes, defy teachers' authority, perform poorly in their grades, bully other learners and bring weapons to school, while academic boys were described as boys who conform to school rules and perform well academically. Being unruly and violent was described as a key marker of being a *tsotsi* boy. Many of the boys confirmed that it was common for boys to fight in the school yard.

Shaun was a creative and talented youngster, who classifed himself as an academic boy. He talked at length about the difficult relationship he had with his father, but he did not allow this to get in the way of the ambitions he had for himself. He had dreams of starting up a youth radio station. When it came to fighting at school, Shaun understood the dynamics: 'Sometimes we feel that if I do not fight they would say that I am weak or I am scared of him. That guy would then take advantage that I did not fight him. He would then look down on me, and say awful things about me.'

William, who never felt very positive about his life circumstances, saw fighting slightly differently. 'So you are proving yourself that, yeah, you can't tell me a thing. I am a man; you can't tell me such things. If you don't fight people will think this one *ke bhari* [fool], you see.'

An increased level of violence has been observed in many South African schools.[3] According to Patrick Burton, one in five school learners is at risk of being bullied, harassed or beaten up at school.[4]

It seems that enhancing their social position was an important factor in adolescent boys' involvement in fights at school. Boys who were unwilling to be violent and who also did not live up to the image of being violent were considered *dibhari* (Sotho word for fools). Self-identified *tsotsi* boys were firmly of the view that reputation and respect were gained only through fights with other boys at school.

The notion of embodying a particular kind of manhood appeared to play a key role in some of the fights that took place in the Alex boys' schools and many of their narratives revealed a perception that willingness to engage in violence was proof of being a 'real' township boy. Thus, violent displays might emerge not only as demonstrations of dominance but also out of a need to achieve or hold onto the hard-won status of being a 'real' township boy. Those boys who either refuse to fight or who get beaten up can lose that status; in this sense they are 'emasculated'. Interestingly, the process of emasculation can occur only if the violence is perpetrated by a male against a male peer.[5] In other words, boys consider other boys worthy opponents to fight against in order to achieve some kind of power and authority. This leads to what Antony Whitehead calls 'heroic masculinity' – the boy who defeats the other is accorded the status of s'khokho (township slang for a hero) and the one who is defeated is seen as an mfana (Sotho word for a little boy).[6] In this respect, tsotsi masculinity is somewhat precarious as it depends on 'weak' male opponents for its confirmation. Dominance has to be constantly reiterated through threats of, or the enactment of, violence against another male. This hero-villain dynamic explains why boys often fight at school because all adolescent boys strive to achieve the status of a hero. Unfortunately, some of these fights are fatal, with boys stabbing each other with sharp objects. Some boys in my study boasted about and took pride in the fights they had had with other boys at school.

In his psychoanalytic study aimed at understanding why young males resort to violence, Duncan Cartwright, in his book, *Psychoanalysis, Violence and Rage-Type Murder: Murdering Minds*, shows that shame and humiliation are central to male violence.[7] Reacting violently is considered a normal response to perceived insults to one's masculinity. It then becomes justified for a boy to 'save face' by fighting back to avoid further humiliation. To emphasise this point, one of the participants in my group stated: 'I need to defend my dignity. You would not want to be told what to do by another boy.' The need to defend one's dignity and to retain the respect of peers seems to be crucial to maintaining a masculine self. In all the interviews, the use of violence was justified as a valid response to other boys' provocations, including fights over girlfriends and inappropriate jokes, such as calling another boy gay (see Chapter 7).

Participants reported that boys who were violent were also defiant against their teachers. They often did not do their schoolwork and missed classes. These boys were also highly disruptive in the classroom and teachers found it difficult to instil any discipline. It seems that tsotsi boys, in many instances, display a public, violent masculine identity as a compensatory mechanism for their lack of academic skills and inability to compete with the academic boys in the classroom.

Simon and Nathan would agree with this view. 'You see, many of these guys [tsotsi boys] are bullies, but failures at school,' said Simon. 'They are failures, you know, when it comes to schoolwork. They get zeros in tests and assignments.' Nathan, for whom schoolwork was important as he had plans to study engineering one day, was not easily impressed by bravado. 'These guys [tsotsi boys] think they are clever, but you know ... I perform better than them in tests and homework. Many fail because they don't study. They only know how to bully other kids ...'

It was reported in the interviews that tsotsi boys generally performed consistently poorly in their schoolwork. It might be speculated that they felt undermined and possibly emasculated in the classroom context. It can therefore be argued that bullying is a tool used by tsotsi boys to render the academic boys powerless, helpless or emasculated outside of the classroom context. In the interviews, tsotsi boys simply justified their involvement in violence as a means of proving their 'manhood', but it is possible that it may also represent, as observed by other researchers, a projection of unwanted feelings of failure, lack, rejection and deprivation.[8]

In talking to the boys who classified themselves as tsotsi boys, it emerged that some felt sad and depressed due to personal problems such as absent parental figures or a lack of structure at home. These emotional problems were then often projected onto other boys at school as a defence mechanism to preserve their fragile sense of self. This suggests that teachers and parents could play an important role in supporting these adolescents in their emotional development and experience. Being violent or defiant at school may in some instances be a cry for help. However, according to William Pollack in his book *Real Boys: Rescuing Our Sons from the Myths*, such behaviour is often misinterpreted as 'boys being boys' and, as a result, nothing is done to help them. There is an argument to be made that rather than seeing tsotsi boys as a problem at school, these are boys who need to be provided with support.

It became clear in the interviews that tsotsi boys constantly felt the need to affirm their positions as 'real' boys. However, the rewards for their public, violent masculine performance appeared to be temporary, leaving them uncertain about what to do next to maintain the same status. A typical trajectory for these boys includes dropping out of school, smoking, experimenting with drugs, and engaging in criminal activities until they are arrested and sentenced. This is the same trajectory that Chandre Gould's *Beaten Bad* revealed about the life stories of prison inmates: many started by bullying other kids at school, dropped out of school and joined local gangs until they were arrested for committing a crime. Some of these problems could be avoided if preventative steps were taken to engage *tsotsi* boys to help them reflect on and think about their violent masculinities and the long-term implications of their behaviours.

*

'Academic boys' are boys who conform to school rules and perform well academically. They are often seen as mature, responsible and studious. Many of these boys reject and subvert the automatic association of masculinity with violence, an otherwise normative view among adolescent boys living in predominantly black townships such as Alexandra. These boys embrace masculine voices that are non-violent, non-risk taking and school oriented.

Tommy was one of them. Even as a schoolboy he showed maturity and a keen sense of self-awareness. He lived with both his parents and two older brothers. His brothers were a significant influence in his life and he looked up to them. He was very focused on his books and the stance of 'education first' was articulated and visibly apparent. He did not seem to mind that he was not especially popular at school and even when he came in for some teasing, particularly when he showed little interest in girls or dating, he shrugged this off easily. 'I just walk away,' he said. 'I just walk away or I try telling the person. If someone's arguing with me I just leave and say okay you're right. I don't like fighting.'

When I asked Tommy whether he wasn't concerned that by walking away he would be laughed at, told he was scared or called a coward, he shook his head. 'I don't look up to people. I'm not interested in what people say,' he said.

'But they will laugh at you,' I pressed.

'Yeah,' he acknowledged, 'but it's not going to be something that's gonna go on forever. They can laugh for that day or the week when they see me but it's not something that can go on forever.'

For Tommy, education was key and he had his eyes firmly on his future. His self-respect was evident and he held himself in high esteem. Peer pressure when it came to drinking and smoking dagga was not something he felt he would easily succumb to – most of the friends he hung out with did not smoke. 'We keep each other in the right frame of mind so we can progress,' he said. Like any other boy growing up, he acknowledged the attraction of material things like expensive cars, clothes, a big house, but he believed that these things could be attained through education, and not only by becoming a gangster.

The desire to do well academically, I realised as I continued with the interviews and made my field notes, was a major protective factor in helping these boys avoid risk-taking behaviours, including violent situations at school. This is in line with Gary Barker's findings among young boys in Brazil and Deevia Bhana's research in South Africa that adolescent males who perform well academically are less likely to be involved in risk-taking behaviours such as gang violence.[9] Additionally, my interviews with the boys highlighted that the academically oriented boys were also less likely to defy teachers' authority. These boys were internally driven to do well in their studies, appeared to have a clear sense of their masculine self and generally displayed a high degree of self-reflection. Their concern was not how they appeared to others, but rather how to reconcile their behaviour with a clear personal identity. They also expressed significantly higher levels of optimism and confidence about the future than their *tsotsi* peers. For example, one of the academic boys said, 'Yeah, we will see who is going to be successful between me and these guys [*tsotsi* boys]. I value my education more than anything.' Having educational aspirations and valuing academic achievement were thus powerful protective factors in helping these boys resist involvement in crime, violence, substance abuse and so on.

Timothy, who was in his last year of high school and looking forward to continuing his education – one of his friends was already studying through the University of South Africa (UNISA), he told me – was all too aware of the dangers of following a wayward lifestyle. 'Believe me,' he said, 'people get killed in some of these fights.' He was one of the few boys in the study who enjoyed a stable family life. A level-headed boy, confident and with a good grasp of who he was, he lived with both his parents and some of his siblings. He saw his brother as a role model and felt that he motivated him to aspire to better things. Sometimes they went shopping together for fancy clothes. His brother owned a home in a smart suburb. '[My brother] has a good job in a big company and now lives the "life"', he said proudly.

Martin was another boy who classified himself as academic. He was shy and reserved in the beginning and did not say much in group sessions. Later he became much more forthcoming, even talkative, and spoke enthusiastically in subsequent years about the experience of being involved in my research project and how it had helped him discover his true self and his identity as a young black man. Early on he was dismissive about what fighting at school said about you. 'I don't think fighting with other boys makes you a "real" boy,' he told me. 'That is for boys that are stupid.'

The academic boys also tended to distance themselves from the violent masculinity commonly associated with township masculinity and were active in carving out alternative, non-violent masculine identities. Boys who classified themselves as 'academic boys' had photos of books in their albums (see figure 7), suggesting the significance of this element of their lives to their identity. They celebrated their studiousness, even though they complained bitterly that they were not as popular as non-academic or *tsotsi* boys. Barker also observed that violent boys often tend to attract popular attention, marginalising those who are non-violent.[10]

Figure 7: One of the academic boys took a photo of books to indicate that reading was important for him.

Tsotsi boys labelled academic boys negatively as 'teachers' pets' or 'Mr Goodboys'. Academic boys were subjected to insults, and teased and called derogatory names such as 'losers' and *snaai* (fools). Academic boys complained that *tsotsi* boys were not only covertly tolerated by teachers, but were also popular with girls. Simon explained it this way: 'But then if you disrespect the teachers you become popular in that group of becoming popular, in that bad way. But then if you play sport, and not being the teacher's pet necessarily, and you [don't] do your homework, you become popular amongst the girls. And the girls would like you that [you are] this guy.'

The academic boys were bewildered by girls' preference for *tsotsi* boys as potential boyfriends. Nathan, whose Christian faith was important to him and who belonged to a youth group, which formed the basis of his socialising, found the attraction of the 'bad boy' puzzling. 'I don't know, these girls of these days,' he complained, 'when they see a boy drinking, smoking and missing classes, they get proud of the boy.'

Despite their commitment to studying and doing well academically, academic boys felt at a disadvantage because they were not generally popular. Simon showed his irritation: '... you don't do your homework but girls would like this,' he said with a sigh.

In their research Frosh and his colleagues found that girls tend to like academic boys because they do not harass or abuse them and they respect teachers, but they do not necessarily like such boys as potential boyfriends.[11] Girls often regard these boys as too effeminate or soft, lacking the key characteristics of conventional adolescent masculinity, such as roughness and toughness.

These findings suggest that there are costs involved in being identified as an academic boy, including being rejected by girls as a potential boyfriend. Girls also tend to see academic boys as boring because they do not go out to parties and are routinely at home reading or doing schoolwork. Nathan spoke about feeling hurt when his girlfriend of two years ended their relationship to go out with a popular *tsotsi* boy at their school. He suspected that he lost her because he was not in the 'cool' group of *tsotsi* boys. Other sacrifices that came with being an academic boy included being bullied and called derogatory names, as alluded to earlier. As a result, some of the boys who classified themselves as 'academic boys' experienced conflicting emotions and considerable ambivalence about their masculine identities, although others appreciated that there were costs and tensions in occupying a mid-hierarchy identity.

'It's like I am that simple guy,' Nathan said. 'I wouldn't say I am popular, I wouldn't say I am a loser. I feel that I am in between.' Simon agreed with this description. 'Yes, being like in between, you wouldn't impress people doing bad things. And again, you wouldn't be that guy that doesn't socialise, like you lock yourself out.'

The complexities of being 'in between' or 'in the borderland' for academic boys were evident and it was something they spoke quite a lot about.[12] They accepted that it was better to be 'in between' and a 'simple guy' who was neither 'popular' nor a 'loser' if this was the cost of having academic aspirations. However, being in the middle constituted a dilemma as they wanted to do well academically but, at the same time, they did not want to be categorised as teachers' pets or bookworms. They wanted to be considered 'real' township boys, doing what other boys did, such as socialising and spending time with peers on street corners, but they also wanted to get good grades at school. This was a difficult balance to achieve. Being an academic boy, therefore, involved the conscious management of their behaviour and the perceptions of others. As Diane Reay puts it, 'to be both academically successful and acceptably male requires a considerable amount of careful negotiation on the part of academic boys'.[13] Like the adolescent boys in Reay's study, academic boys in my study were also caught between two opposing positions in attempting to ensure that their sufficiently tough and socially integrated township masculinities were kept intact, while simultaneously endeavouring to maintain their academic success. This internal and external battle was a constant one, which many of the academic boys had to manage in order to be seen as 'real' township boys. In the interviews, a number of them spoke about studying privately at home or in secret places, such as the library in town, so as not to attract negative attention from other boys, and girls.

According to my study's findings, *tsotsi* boys were at the top of the masculine hierarchy in the school context. They were seen as the 'coolest' and most popular group by the majority of boys who took part in the project. Some of the other boys, including academic boys, strove to be like them without compromising their studies, although a few were willing to forfeit their schoolwork by adhering to the norms of *tsotsi* masculinity. Academic boys employed various coping strategies, such as also at times fooling around in the classroom, in order to be in the 'cool' group. One academic boy said, 'I was playing in class, neglecting my schoolwork, yeah, you see, making jokes about teachers in order to be "cool".' Peer pressure is thus exerted on adolescent boys to belong to certain cliques at school, but this comes at a price that may involve neglecting schoolwork in order to be accepted by the in-group. Adolescent boys who do not comply with particular masculine practices are refused membership of these groups.[14]

Academic boys found themselves in a dilemma because they wanted to belong to the 'cool' group but, simultaneously, questioned some behaviours associated with *tsotsi* masculinity, such as missing classes or not doing their schoolwork. They were thus forced to negotiate conflicting voices of masculinity and felt uncertain about their subjective positions. As a result, academic boys employed a range of discursive and behavioural strategies to legitimise themselves, such as identifying with and belonging to several groups or cliques rather than confining themselves to one group.

Herman was a good example. Tall and good-looking, he carried himself with confidence and talked in a loud voice, often making jokes and making the other boys laugh. He had a great sense of humour which, I think, stood him in good stead. He happily acknowledged that he was 'in between', a boy who worked at his school tasks and wanted to do well academically but a boy who also did what *tsotsi* boys did, such as teasing teachers, 'just to be cool', but not in an extreme way. He was comfortable not belonging to a single group – publicly, he acted as something of a *tsotsi* boy, but at the same time he did not neglect his schoolwork.

This approach, which could be seen as a 'face-saving' strategy, was also employed by some of the other academic boys, in order to maintain their school-oriented masculinity while simultaneously embracing certain practices of *tsotsi* masculinity. Through this strategy, they could straddle positions as both outsider and insider without being seen as inferior and inadequate. These 'in betweeners' were accepted in the worlds of *tsotsi* boys as well as among academic boys. Wayne Martino and Maria Pallotta-Chiarolli found that academically oriented adolescent boys in Australia employed similar strategies to deal with bullies at school.[15]

Academic boys who moved between groups and occupied multiple positions were also less likely to be bullied because they had the cultural and social capital to negotiate boundaries between groups without being seen as easy targets. It is conceivably less emotionally taxing for an academic boy to occupy multiple positions simultaneously since this allows for social integration and the avoidance of denigration. However, some of the boys in the study experienced being in the borderland as emotionally draining and frustrating. One academic boy said, 'I hate to pretend. I just want to be myself.' The emotional toll of pretending to be something they were not was echoed by other academic boys. They felt they were being dishonest to their 'real' selves for the sake of wanting to be seen as 'cool'. Aligning themselves with a *tsotsi* identity thus had both costs and benefits for academic boys as they attempted to position themselves as academic but not marginalised.

Nevertheless, some of the academic boys felt confident enough to reject the dominant norms of *tsotsi* boys without feeling the need to straddle or occupy multiple positions. These boys were aware of the peer pressure to conform to certain practices but were able to deal with their peers' negative input. Themba, for example, managed to maintain a balance by playing sport – improving his already excellent soccer skills – but also paying attention to his studies. When *tsotsi* boys teased him by calling him a bookworm, he would console himself by thinking: 'Let's put five years down the line and see what is going to happen; who is going to be a bookworm, who is going to wash whose car, who is going to be whose garden boy ...'

Themba seemed to cope well and managed to resist peer pressure to engage in anti-school behaviours such as missing classes or defying teachers. He saw education as an investment for the future. He believed that although he might currently occupy an inferior position, he would be in a superior position later in his life, when *tsotsi* boys would be working as his servants, washing his car and working as 'garden boys' at his home. In his album, he had a photo of a Mercedes Benz and a big house (see figure 8).

Figure 8: The Mercedez Benz 'dream car' was a new model at the time the photo was taken in 2007.

Because of his dreams for his future, Themba was highly motivated to do well at school. He completed his matric and, at the time of writing, was working as an IT specialist.

Many of the academic boys in the study were future oriented and because of this were willing to forgo peer approval in the present in order to achieve their future aspirations. They saw pursuing academic work as an investment in the future and as a possible means to break the cycle of poverty in their lives.

Adolescent boys' status, it seems, is derived from holding or being ascribed a certain position within the peer group hierarchy. The subjective positions that academic boys occupy, therefore, are fluid rather than rigid and fixed. They vacillate between multiple positions, simultaneously accepting and rejecting certain practices of township masculinity. As a result, they have conflicting feelings about identifying with alternative voices of masculinity. Some want to be popular and yet still achieve good grades at school. They have to manage these contradictions in order to maintain and sustain emerging alternative school-oriented voices of masculinity. Being a 'different' boy in this 'in between' space is a complex process, characterised by feelings of anxiety, hesitation and ambivalence.

6 | Double Standards – Dating, Sex and Girls

With regard to sexual identity and heterosexual engagement, what became clear to me as our interviews progressed was that adolescent boys' voices reflect conflicts and contradictions in their construction of masculinity.

All of the 32 boys who began this research project with me and went off for two weeks with their disposable cameras came back with photos of girls to put in their albums. In the individual as well as group interviews, they spent a lot of time talking about their relationships with girls. They said that it was important for a boy to have a girlfriend, but expectations in terms of these relationships differed from one boy to another. Many said they expected to have sex with multiple girlfriends as sexual relations were seen as a key marker of successful township masculinity. This prioritising of sex with multiple girlfriends was rejected by some boys, however, which indicated to me that not all boys are interested in having sex with (multiple) girls. An alternative masculinity, one that promotes 'faithfulness' in relationships with girls and challenges popular misogynistic views of girls as sex objects appears, as elsewhere, to be emerging in a township environment too. These boys said they believed that girls should be treated with respect and dignity. There is some way to go, but it is this view that we need to promote in the mainstream.

It has to be said that this view was not the popular consensus among the majority of the boys I interviewed, but what was indisputable was that girls were a central topic of discussion for all the boys. Having multiple sexual partners came up regularly. It was described as a key marker of being a *sex-jaro* (slang term for boys who like to have sex with many different girls).

Martin, who was one of the boys who most enjoyed the photo-taking part of the project and took it very seriously, said the following about *sex-jaro* boys. 'This guy,' he said, pointing to a photo he had taken at school,

> this guy is *sex-jaro*. A *sex-jaro* is a boy who likes girls. Like '*jaro*'; '*jaro*' never fails in anything. There is no girl who can say no to him when he chats her up. He can get a girl any time whenever he wants. He can do anything he wants to do at that moment, and no one would tell him anything. So that is why I tell you that this boy dates a girl today and then the next day he wants to have sex with her. So they are called *sex-jaros*.

Multiple examples of *sex-jaro* boys were given in the interviews. *Sex-jaro* boys seem to have a lot in common with the *ingangara* boys identified in Terry-Ann Selikow, Bheki Zulu and Eugene Cedras' study.[1] They have a sense of superiority when it comes to chasing and dating girls. According to Martin and other boys, '*sex-jaros* never fail in winning the girl over'. Their ultimate goal is to make a sexual conquest as quickly as possible – to date a girl for one day and then to have sex with her the next day. In their lingo, the boys call this kind of pursuit 'go shaya shaya' (telling a girl a lot of lies in order to have sex with her within a short space of time). This is regarded as a special skill, possessed only by *sex-jaro* boys. *Sex-jaro* boys also take pride in the number of conquests they are able to make, as illustrated in one of my interviews with Timothy, at 18, a self-identified *sex-jaro* boy:

'How many girlfriends do you have?'

'A lot,' he replied. 'I can't even count them for you.' He laughed at the expression on my face. I noted that he was not in his school uniform today, but wearing a brand-name T-shirt and new-looking sneakers, perhaps a result of one of his shopping trips with his older brother.

'What is a lot?' I asked. 'More than five?'

He laughed again. 'Five is too little,' he said.

'More than eight?' I guessed.

'Eight is too few,' he said, then clarified: 'I've been dating for a long time.'

I waited and then he continued: 'I don't even know how many girls I've dated ever since I got here. I make sure that every year in my class I have a girlfriend and it happens.'

In Timothy's eyes, having had more than eight girlfriends over his life as a teen was an achievement worth celebrating. He was boastful in the interview and clearly amused at my ignorance in expecting him to have had only one or a limited number. *Sex-jaro* boys play a 'numbers game', he explained; they compete with each other to see who has the most girl-friends and who has slept with the most girls. This is similar to the findings in a study conducted in Soweto township by Selikow, Zulu and Cedras, which revealed that a group of sexually active adolescent boys kept a reg-ister of their sexual conquests pinned on their walls and ran a competition to see who could sleep with the most girls each week. A boy who slept with multiple girlfriends was either seen as a 'real' *sex-jaro* or as an *ingangara*.

The *sex-jaro* narratives that emerged in the interviews that came to shape my book strongly suggested that girls were treated primarily as sex objects or conquests by these boys; they described their relationships with girls only in terms of sex. The boys' perception was that they could not live without sex and that it was part of 'male nature' to seek regular sex with multiple partners. They asserted that it was boring to have sex with only one partner. They all boasted about having had sex with more than one girl.

Some of the narratives highlighted the importance of disclosing to male peers one's sexual success with multiple girlfriends. This seemed to enhance *sex-jaro* boys' public status and acceptability. They were seen as role models by their male peers and admired for the fact that they had been able to engage in sexual relations with many girls. It was evident that disclosing their sexual escapades boosted adolescent boys' status in the male peer group.

Successful masculinity included not only the ability to secure multiple sexual partners, but also the ability to perform adequately sexually and to give girls satisfaction. All the *sex-jaro* boys contended that their manhood was tested during sex, a point emphasised by Timothy: 'You do it [sexual activity] right so that you can keep her for [a] long period of time, but if you don't do it right she would leave you and look for someone that can do better than you.' This highlights Timothy's concern about possibly failing to satisfy his multiple girlfriends sexually, which would bring feelings of shame and a sense of inadequacy. *Sex-jaro* boys are expected to be sexually experienced. In one group interview, a very explicit and lively discussion, the boys engaged in competitive talk about who was best able to satisfy a girlfriend sexually. They took turns mentioning that it was important for boys to 'massage' and engage in foreplay activities in order to satisfy their girlfriends sexually.

'What is it that you discuss?' I asked.

William, whose doom and gloom attitude to life sometimes made him monosyllabic, grew animated when he talked about his multiple girlfriends. 'Like when it comes to satisfying a girl, massaging and doing foreplay,' he said.

'You've got to know the G-spot,' Themba volunteered, 'clitoris and stuff. We talk of certain positions. We just talk!'

'Okay,' I said. 'Is it important for a boy to satisfy a girl sexually?'

'Yes,' Themba said firmly, 'it is important to satisfy a girl sexually.'

'To be in the crowd it is. To be that popular boy, it is,' said Oupa, another self-identified *sex-jaro* boy.

However, these boys also seemed to experience some fears and anxieties that they might not be able to meet their partners' desires. Masculinity was associated with sexual adequacy, suggesting that adolescent boys may be under considerable pressure to be sexually experienced or at least to appear to be so. Sex was constructed as a masculine-driven act and failure to satisfy girlfriends was one of the most forceful indictments of masculine power. This is in keeping with the observations of other gender scholars.[2]

Satisfying girls sexually was a key marker of being a 'real' *sex-jaro* boy, but Timothy expressed a concern in the interview that 'some [boys] do it to satisfy their own sexual needs'. He criticised these boys for being selfish in thinking only about satisfying their own sexual needs and ignoring those of girls. In his narrative, he advised his male peers to think about girls' sexual needs, arguing that sex was not a one-sided activity. He maintained that both parties should enjoy sex equally because 'it is all about putting both interests to heart'. In some respects, this aspect of the discussion ran counter to the notion of sex as conquest and as a kind of collection of trophies, with girls being duped and seduced rather than engaged with as sexual partners who have their own needs and desires. *Sex-jaro* boys who entertained these somewhat more egalitarian views about sex seemed to challenge traditional notions of masculinity – that sex is all about penetration and male orgasm. William said he and his friends shared sexual tips such as the importance of touching girls' erogenous zones to ensure that they experienced sexual satisfaction. It is possible that there was considerable posturing in these group interviews, as *sex-jaro* boys were invested in presenting an image of themselves as 'macho', sexually competent and potent. Their references to body parts and sexual practices, and the need for sensitivity to the pleasuring of girls, appeared to be designed, at least in part, to impress their peers and to shore up their confidence in this area. However, it became evident in the follow-up individual interviews I conducted with them that many *sex-jaro* boys were privately worried about their ability to satisfy girls sexually.

As described in her book *Slow Motion: Changing Masculinities, Changing Men*, Lynne Segal found in her research that men generally worry about their ability to satisfy their partners sexually, revealing something artificial or fragile about males' 'macho' hypersexual image. A woman who expresses dissatisfaction with her male partner's sexual performance may cause a major narcissistic injury to his sense of manhood.

Timothy seemed to bear this out, admitting that he would be hurt if his girlfriend said she did not enjoy sex with him. Non-enjoyment would undermine his *sex-jaro* identity because *sex-jaro* boys are publicly expected to be 'experts' on issues of sex and sexual performance. This is consistent with Segal's contention that while sex for males is a source of pleasure and power, it simultaneously produces feelings of self-doubt. The *sex-jaro* boys in my study appeared to experience these fears and anxieties. This also emerged in one of the group interviews where the participants bragged about the size of their penises, evoking hegemonic phallic notions of the bigger, the harder, the better. A big penis was considered a symbol of sexual strength. It was interesting that some boys compared a penis with a gun, in keeping with Chris Dolan's argument that a gun in this context is not just a gun – it is a symbol of power, authority and masculine pride.[3] Many of the adolescent boys also believed that they had to have a big penis (hence all the adverts for penis enlargement in the inner city of Johannesburg and surrounding townships, including Alex) and be able to maintain a firm and lasting erection without early ejaculation in order to satisfy their partners.

Both the group and individual interviews elicited material indicating that adolescent boys might benefit from sex education, including education that questions traditional notions of masculinity as being based on sexual performance.

*

One theme that emerged in the individual interviews I conducted with *sex-jaro* boys was their fear and anxiety about intimate relationships with only one sexual partner. The fear centred on the possibility of girls leaving them and was part of their justification for engaging in several relationships simultaneously.

Soft-spoken Peter, who spent time thinking about and talking through issues of gender equality, had an interesting way of justifying having two girlfriends.

'You must not look up to one girl,' he pronounced. 'Look up to two girls – because if you have one, when she leaves you, you are going to be left with nothing.'

'Why is it not possible to have one girlfriend?' I asked him.

'Most of your organs are in pairs,' he explained, 'which means you have to have two girlfriends.' He paused and looked at me.

'What do you mean when you say most of your organs are in pairs?' I asked.

'Like you have two eyes, two nostrils, two ears and two hands,' he said, holding up his hands to demonstrate. 'So they say even a bicycle has two wheels. So you must also have many girlfriends to avoid any disappoint[ment] if she leaves.'

I put the same question – Is it not possible to have one girlfriend? – to the academic Shaun, one of the boys who was especially energetic in the project and did a lot to encourage other boys to take part. He was always thinking ahead and making plans for different scenarios.

'I do not want to rely on one person,' he told me. 'When she tells me that it's over, I would not have that stress to even hang myself or kill myself over her. So by having another girlfriend, when she tells me that it's over, I know that I have a back-up plan.'

As their rationales illustrate, both boys justified their need to have more than one girlfriend out of a fear of being hurt or abandoned. It seems boys perhaps feel more insecure and vulnerable in relationships than might be evident at face value, but they conceal this fear by having multiple girlfriends. It is possible that these boys' fear of intimacy and the anxiety associated with any dependence is split off and projected onto girls, who are viewed as untrustworthy. Given these boys' acknowledgement of their own sexual non-fidelity, characterising girls in this way may well represent a projection of their own fear to commit. According to Candida Yates, the defensive psychic mechanisms of splitting and projection are regularly used by boys to deny the more vulnerable aspects of the self, which are then projected onto girls as a means of protecting the ideal masculine ego.[4]

Many of the boys in my study justified having multiple partners by accusing girls of being uncommitted and undependable, which, on closer analysis of their narratives, appeared to be untrue. Having multiple partners gave *sex-jaro* boys a sense of power and control. However, the fear of disintegration following the break-up of a relationship revealed something important about the fragility of *sex-jaro* masculinity, necessitating a 'back-up plan' to obviate any potential pain and mourning after a possible failed relationship. It is evident that boys or men in general find it difficult to talk about their hurt feelings following the dissolution of a relationship, especially if the break-up is as a result of the female partner's infidelity, which impacts negatively on their sense of manhood. These are some of the toxic masculine discourses, including conceptions of intimate relations, which we need to challenge among adolescent boys and men in general.

It was evident in this study that boys are expected to cheat on girls but not the other way around. Girls are expected to be faithful and to demonstrate high levels of commitment in relationships. It is seen as the male's prerogative to start or end a relationship and girls who take over this agency undermine adolescent boys' masculinity. In Deevia Bhana and Bronwynne Anderson's study, some girls claimed that because boys were not faithful, there was no reason for them to be loyal and faithful either, indicating an awareness on their part of double standards in gendered heterosexual relationships.[5] In retaliation, boys use violence or vulgar language, including derogatory names such *difebe* (bitches), against girls who decide to date multiple partners as boys do. It appears that boys set the standard for acceptable behaviour, which includes the expectation that girls should not take the initiative in heterosexual relationships, should not ask boys out on a date and must be faithful in relationships. Boys in this study labelled girls who made themselves easily sexually available as 'loose' or whores, but, at the same time, they did not like girls who 'played too hard to get'.

On this point, Mindy Stombler contends that boys give girls mixed messages about 'proper' sexual behaviour because they expect them to be sexually available, but not too easily available – girls are thus expected to perform a balancing act.[6] It became clear, based on the Alex boys' narratives, that girls and women are denied independence in directing their sex lives and freely expressing their sexual desires. Girls are told that they cannot decide when and how to have sex. Thus their dilemma is to maintain the reputation of being a 'good' girl rather than a 'whore' and at the same time not to be seen as withholding or playing too hard to get. Unlike boys, who publicly boast about their multiple partners, girls have to be discreet because they risk being assaulted if their boyfriends find out that they have been unfaithful.[7] Boys discredit and undermine girls' right to have multiple partners. Elmien Lesch and Lou-Marie Kruger as well as Deevia Bhana and Bronwynne Anderson argue that adolescent girls should be empowered to assert their rights as sexual beings and to celebrate their sexuality, as adolescent boys do.[8] *Sex-jaro* boys in the study felt justified in using girls as sex objects and having sex with different partners while denying girls the same freedom. Such double standards endorse male supremacy and, in this study, resulted in adolescent boys actively policing girls' behaviour, for example by ostracising and labelling them negatively if they did not conform to the expected gender norms. Such domination of girls is collectively rationalised and reinforced, indicating how masculine identity is expressed as sexual proactivity and prowess, while at the same time being guarded and protected.

*

Sex-jaro boys spoke proudly about having sexual relations with both steady girlfriends and *makwapeng* (Sotho word for secret lovers), who were treated differently. William, who was 16 years old at the time I met him and a self-identified *sex-jaro* boy and, by his own admission smoked and drank to excess, argued that a steady girlfriend is not treated in the same way as a secret lover.

'I have other girlfriends,' he said in an interview, meaning girls he had sex with.

'With them, does the same principle apply about no sex?' I asked, to be sure that I understood.

'I have had sex with them,' he replied.

'Why with them and not her [his steady girlfriend]?' I pressed.

'You see with these girls [secret lovers] is because of their mentality. They like bad things. They are in the fast lane. We do what we do but not with her. She [his steady girlfriend] is someone I want to build a family with her. I can't afford to lose her over them.'

'With them, do you also talk to them about things like safe sex?'

'No, with them is all about sex, but my girlfriend we talk about everything, including HIV and AIDS and condom use.'

As William explained it to me, this suggests that secret lovers are treated exclusively as sex objects because with them 'it is all about sex'. When it came to his steady girlfriend, however, William wanted to 'build a family with her' and therefore abstained from full sexual relations. The feminist writer Jane Ussher has referred to this as the 'Madonna and whore syndrome', where girls are cast into opposite categories by boys – either as Madonnas (an idealised, romanticised representation of a woman, in this case a steady girlfriend) or as whores (a woman who is seen as sexually loose, in this case a secret lover).[9] All the boys asserted that there was no bonding or emotional connection with secret lovers. They 'positioned' their secret lovers as being in the 'fast lane' and liking 'bad things' and, as a result, the relationships with them were about sex and nothing else.

Some boys disclosed that they did not use condoms in some of their sexual encounters. They all acknowledged that they knew about HIV and AIDS and how to prevent transmission of the virus, but it seems this knowledge did not generally influence them to change their risky sexual practices. Researchers have for many years asked why so many adolescents still engage in unsafe sexual practices when they know that these practices may result in HIV infection. In their HIV prevention work with South African youth, Catherine Campbell, Catherine MacPhail, Deevia Bhana, Rachel Jewkes and Robert Morrell concluded that the *context* of adolescents should be taken into account when trying to understand lifestyle choices that place young people at risk of infection.[10] As noted earlier, sexually active boys are seen as 'cool'. However, achieving this status comes at a price, which may involve risking one's health or life. This kind of risk taking is exaggerated among adolescents, given their developmental stage and the resulting impressionableness. It is important, therefore, to create safe spaces in which to engage with adolescents about these risk-taking behaviours. Such conversations should be non-judgemental and allow boys to express their views, fears, anxieties and stressors in their personal lives, including the non-use of condoms. After my follow-up interviews with them, some boys showed a willingness to reconsider and rethink their risky sexual behaviours. They were more reflective about these behaviours, without boasting or performing the *sex-jaro* role.

Not all boys engage in risky sexual behaviours, however, and some of those in my study were critical of *sex-jaro* boys' risky sexual practices. Nigel Edley and Margaret Wetherell identify such boys as occupying a 'rebellious' subject position in which the macho and risky sexual behaviours of other boys are rejected and challenged.[11] All the Alex boys who rejected the idea of multiple partners were academically oriented and, as noted, this was a protective factor against involvement in risk-taking behaviours. Academic boy Simon took the moral position that boys should not tell girls that they loved them while knowing that they were betraying them by having other relationships. His main complaint was that having multiple partners, lying and seeing sex as a priority in relationships tarnished the image of 'good' boys like him because girls then saw all boys in the same light ('boys only want sex'). This view was supported by other academic boys, who also rejected 'this thing of having two girls or more'. They argued that boys should be 'faithful' or abstain.

*

Ten boys in the study disclosed in the individual interviews with me that they were virgins. This was surprising, not only because it seemed unusual for adolescent boys to disclose such intimate information, but also because the prevalent view is that adolescent boys are sexually active. Unlike the *sex-jaro* boys, these participants contended that boys should abstain from sex until they are older.

Nathan was one of those who had a girlfriend but was content to wait. 'She is special in many ways,' he said. 'I love her a lot, and I wish that I could end up with her. And I feel comfortable when I am with her. We haven't had sex and I'm happy with that.' He was clearly proud to be a virgin, rejecting the view that boys *must* have sex or multiple partners. Thabiso, too, who lived with his grandmother, said he was happy about his decision not to have sex until he was married. He contended that it was worthwhile to 'sign the contract with yourself' not to have sex until the right moment. He was artistic and had dreams of becoming a cartoonist one day.

Herman, always neat in his school uniform, and energetically involved in peer group activities and not easily influenced by other boys, was clear about his subjective masculine position. 'I have a girl-friend because I love her and nothing else. I do not go with other guys who want to impress their friends and to have sex with the girl. I am not doing it because of that.' For Herman, having a girlfriend was all about love and 'nothing else'. Unlike *sex-jaro* boys, he did not harbour an ulterior motive – pursuing girls purely as sexual conquests or trophies – for wanting a relationship. He looked down on *sex-jaro* boys who had sex with girls to impress their male counterparts. He saw this as stupid, despite the fact that he was ridiculed by *sex-jaro* boys at school. 'The other guys were saying I am a fool, I do not want ... I only want to have girls for the fun; I do not have sex with them. That is what the other boys were saying.'

The boys who were happy still to be virgins acknowledged that it wasn't an easy decision because they were teased and ridiculed and some of them had mixed feelings about their decision; sometimes these feelings caused emotional tensions.

It was generally the academic boys who were more likely than others to abstain from sexual relations, and some of these identified themselves as Christian. Not having sex before marriage, they explained, was part of their religious beliefs and that was one of the reasons they abstained. One of the boys included in his photographs narrative a picture he'd taken during a camp that was organised by his church. He said religion played a key role in helping him cope with some of the challenges of being an adolescent. This was a view that was shared by other boys.

Figure 9: This photo, taken by one of the boys during a church camp, was intended to highlight that he was Christian.

These Christian boys spoke openly about being teased and ridiculed as *dikgope* (Sotho word for a boy who does not have a girlfriend and has never had sex). Some who disclosed that they were virgins spoke about feeling pressurised to have girlfriends and sexual relationships, but they were able to resist these pressures, despite it not being easy. 'Being a Christian boy is a tough battle,' Simon admitted. Many of the Christian boys mentioned that they often experienced confusion and uncertainty due to the teasing they endured daily from the other boys, especially *sex-jaro* boys, because they had never had sex.

Hierarchically, the Christian boys apparently occupied the second to bottom position (with gay boys occupying the bottom position) in terms of adolescent boys' status on the masculine hierarchy in Alexandra. Christian boys tended to be ridiculed as 'fools' and were insulted by being called belittling terms such as *umzalwana* (the Zulu word for being a Christian, but in this context used derogatorily to refer to someone who goes to church regularly and believes sex before marriage is a sin). Being ridiculed as *umzalwana* evoked in them feelings of hurt and discrimination.

The Christian boys used their religious beliefs as a protective coping mechanism to resist, reject and subvert popular norms of *sex-jaro* masculinity. They also seemed to have developed a clear sense of self to deal with the derogatory names thrown at them. Some boys, like Nathan, for example, were not bothered by the insults, and were also confident enough in their identities not to be influenced by their peers to engage in risk-taking behaviours. 'Other boys [especially *sex-jaro* boys] used to say bad things about me,' Nathan said. 'Call me *umzalwana*, that I like going to church. But as a human being I do not take what they say personally.'

These boys' affirmation and validation were internally driven rather than based primarily on external loci of control, although their sense of belonging to a congregation of Christian people probably helped to shore up this identity. However, the Christian boys generally experienced internal battles and the theme of managing the temptation to have sexual relations emerged strongly in the interviews with boys who mainly self-identified as Christian. For example, Simon spoke about coping strategies he used to deal with some of his internal conflicts. He claimed that being a Christian helped him handle a range of 'temptations', including the temptation to have sex. He told me in a one-on-one interview session about a particular occasion when he had been tempted to have sex with his girlfriend but it didn't happen.

'I was home alone, and then I brought my girlfriend inside the house; and then actually, like, my sister came in and then she just found me. I was in the kitchen. I was, like, pouring some juice, biscuits and all that. And I think that was, like … I think it was the way it was meant to happen. And I was meant to do what I was thinking in my mind to please other people. I think my sister was meant to come in at that time.'

'But if your sister didn't come in?' I said. 'Were you then going to have sex with the girl?'

Simon paused, thinking. 'Yeah, I was just going to do it,' he sighed. 'And then afterwards you've got that pleasure – afterwards you're going to your friends. Yeah, I had sex with this girl.'

Although Simon had obviously been in two minds about whether to have sex with his girlfriend or not, he seemed pleased that he had abstained. He did acknowledge, however, that if his sister had not returned, he may well have broken his no-sex rule. Interestingly, the anticipated pleasure associated with potentially having sex seems to have been as much about sharing the experience with other boys as it was about the sexual act itself. This reinforces the notion that masculine identity is intricately tied up with making one's prowess public, even if only to a limited group of friends. However, Simon maintained that it was possible for a boy to be a virgin and still retain his masculine identity. He claimed that it was unacceptable for a Christian boy to have sex before marriage as this contravened the teachings of Christianity.

In sum, religious beliefs, teachings and mores may help adolescent boys to exercise self-control in abstaining from sexual activity.[12] However, the process of managing oneself in relation to this kind of prohibition seemed for Simon and some of the other boys in the study who identified as Christian to be anxiety provoking and even threatening.

Simon's views were similar to those of 17-year-old Michael, who also classified himself as a Christian. Michael was a member of a well-known charismatic church in Randburg and he was very involved in church activities. He was a youth pastor and sang in the choir. He wasn't especially popular at school, but this did not bother him unduly, he said. Within his church and the group activities linked to it, he was well liked and fulfilled. Like Simon, he also had his own internal battles. Temptations would always be there, he said, but in terms of his religious beliefs sex before marriage was a sin. He had to convince himself that 'it is wrong, it is wrong' and after he had had one of these internal dialogue/self-talks, he was able to control himself. However, sometimes the temptations became too strong for him to deal with alone and then he turned to his church. 'I consult someone who's like an elder at church, like sister P. I don't just deal with them myself because sometimes I'll deal with them and then I take the wrong decisions or choices, and then it ends up being a mix-up.'

In Michael's case, the resources were available for him to talk about his feelings and conflicts as there was a support system for him at the church. The church elders seemed quite prepared to talk to teenagers about their life struggles. Michael told me he always consulted sister P at church about his life problems, including temptations to experiment sexually.

Martin, another Christian, said that Alexandra township had too many temptations, such as 'parties on weekends and seeing boys and girls hugging and kissing in public'. He was all too aware of how one could take a wrong path and get into trouble – his brother was addicted to drugs, which was a source of pain to him and his mother. (Martin was one of the few boys whose photo album included a picture of his mother.) He was a slightly chubby boy and his natural shyness meant that he didn't have many close friends. He also experienced contradictory emotions about his decision to abstain sexually and the temptations a party environment presented. He described to me a predicament in which he had found himself one weekend: 'I was at a house party so the majority of boys were having sex, but the girl that I was standing with ... and we were just drinking cooldrink ... That was it, okay! She said what about moving out from what they were doing and then go and stay outside and talk about something? So I realised that there are different people because if it were someone else she would also want to do it. She showed me how truthful she was that I am too young and I am too special. I'll never do this thing.'

Martin was tempted to have sex but was relieved that he managed to retain his integrity as a Christian, in part because of the support of the girl he was with. I wondered how Martin would have reacted had this girl shown an interest in having sex with him. All the boys who had never had sex acknowledged that the desire to have sex was always present. They reported that they engaged in a process of self-talk or internal dialogue to manage the desire. For example, to control his sexual feelings, Martin said, 'I talk to myself and say it is wrong to have sex.' Michael said that he often prayed to control his sexual urges.

Judging by Simon's, Nathan's, Michael's and Martin's narratives, being a 'different' boy in respect of abstaining from sex was clearly difficult. Their subjective positioning was characterised by feelings of ambivalence and having to negotiate alternative voices of masculinity in respect of whether or not to seek out and engage in sexual intercourse. They repressed their sexual desires, fearing that if they were unchecked they would run out of control. In this respect, although they renounced sexual engagement, their talk supported 'the male sexual drive' discourse in that they seemed to subscribe to a construction of themselves (and other boys) as naturally and strongly desirous of sex. Simon's, Martin's and Michael's narratives revealed that their sexual feelings were not always successfully repressed. This is because repression is a contradictory defence mechanism – it is always related to desire and ends in an intense internal struggle. The repression of sexual desire produced feelings of anxiety in some of these boys, once again showing that masculine subjects are not homogeneous in their identities. Since sexual material was socially and religiously unacceptable to the conscious minds of the Christian boys, their 'self' was split into two: a desiring part and a restraining part; the 'naturally' sexed boy versus the Christian virgin. They relied heavily on their internal Christian 'voices' to manage the temptation to have sex. As was evident, the Christian boys were more likely than non-Christian boys, such as *sex-jaro* boys, to delay their sexual debut. Christianity thus seemed to be a positive protective factor in helping adolescent boys to resist peer pressure to have early and non-committed sexual relationships, and perhaps, by implication, to refrain from engaging in other risky behaviours.

All of those who were virgins agreed that it was not easy to tell other boys that they had never had sex; this was information they kept private. Interestingly, many only disclosed their virgin status to me in the follow-up individual interviews. It is possible that the participants felt more at ease with me by that time, enabling them to share material about more sensitive topics. As mentioned earlier, the follow-up individual interviews enhanced the rapport between me and the participants in that I was apparently seen as a 'trusted' male figure who could contain their fears and keep their 'shameful' secrets confidential.

Many of them felt pressured to lie about their sexual involvement in order to prove their virility. Lying about one's sexual history may manifest in what Janet Holland, Caroline Ramazanoglu, Sue Sharpe and Rachel Thomson call telling 'public performance stories', where young men recount fabricated sexual experiences in order to project an image of being a 'macho, knowing and experienced male'.[13]

David had a different take on why he played up his sexual experience when in the company of his friends. He was a good-looking boy with a wide smile and engaging personality. 'What I try to do is ... I will join their conversation and we'd discuss, just so that they should not think that I am side-lining myself. Because if I can start asking questions, they will think that I am gay.' In fact David had never had sex with his girlfriend, but when he was with his male friends he pretended to be experienced. He participated in boys' sex talk and lied about his sexual experience because he did not want his male peers to think he was inexperienced sexually but also because he didn't want to be thought gay. His narrative shows that boys scrutinise and police each other in respect of their accounts of sexual prowess, which can lead to posturing and lying. David wasn't the only one who voiced the fear of being considered gay. Being considered gay had many negative connotations for the participants because homosexuality was seen as a deviation from the commonly accepted and prescribed masculine practice of heterosexuality.

Being seen as unmanly, whether as gay, a virgin or a Christian, evoked fear in many of the Alex boys in my study. In these kinds of contexts, boys may well engage in compensatory masculine activities, such as being promiscuous or at least pretending that they are, to affirm themselves as members of the male club. Fabricating or exaggerating one's sexual experience is also an important part of the 'public performance' of complying with the hegemonic views of a *sex-jaro*-type masculinity. Those who tell the truth about their lack of sexual experience are seen as 'fools' for failing in the masculine task of sexual conquest and prowess. They are viewed as at risk, not only socially but also in terms of their physical and psychological health. The male sexual drive discourse had strong currency among all the boys, both those who engaged in sex and boasted about multiple and even high-risk encounters, and those who refrained from sex and expressed the need for strong self-control in this regard.

It is apparent, therefore, that the demonstration of sexual prowess is central to young male identity. The pressure to perform in this way, or at least to appear to perform, means that it is quite common for boys to exaggerate or fabricate tales of their sexual encounters in the company of other boys.

7 | Defying Homophobia: 'This is Who I am, Finish and *Klaar*'

Many township boys appear to be internally threatened by and conflicted about the apparent 'unmanliness' associated with gay masculinity.

Besides talking about girls, all the boys who participated in my study spent a lot of time talking about 'gay' boys.[1] It was quickly apparent through our discussions, particularly the group discussions, that boys who failed to live up to the norms of heterosexual masculinity, like other boys who did not live up to the norms of hegemonic masculinity, were ostracised, ridiculed and called derogatory names such as 'sissies' or *isitabane* (Zulu word for gay). Many of the boys felt threatened by the perceived 'unmanliness' associated with 'gay' masculinity. In order to maintain their 'straight' masculinity, all the boys reported that they isolated themselves from 'gay' boys and avoided practices or behaviours that could be associated with homosexuality.[2] A major theme that emerged in the interviews was the characterisation of same-sex relations as un-Christian, sexually aberrant, perverse, contaminating and threatening to the institution of the heterosexual family. The boys' responses reflected little tolerance of same-sex relations despite the existence of gay-sympathetic constitutional rights in South Africa and considerable change in social attitudes to homosexuality globally.

In the interviews they employed various discourses (for example medical, religious and psychological) to justify their discrimination against gay boys at school. All the boys (*tsotsi* boys, *sex-jaro* boys, academic boys and Christian boys) classified themselves as straight. Only two participants classified themselves as gay, although at the time of our first interviews in 2007 one of them was not yet out of the closet. He only disclosed to me two years later, in 2009, that he was gay.

In the pecking order, gay boys were 'othered'. They were at the bottom of the masculine hierarchy. All of the boys appreciated the need to behave in a particular manner to avoid accusations of being gay, suggesting that 'gayness' was not defined purely on the basis of same-sex sexual desire or relationships, but also associated with other stereotypically defined practices and behaviours. All the boys mentioned the fear of being seen as gay as a major concern, signalling that same-sex relations presents a threat to adolescent boys' sense of manhood. This for me reveals the subtle and somewhat contradictory power that gay masculinity holds in relation to straight masculinity.

All the boys in the study described the discrimination against 'gay' boys at school as necessary and justifiable. In order to maintain their straight masculinity, they distanced themselves from gay boys, leaving these boys socially isolated.

In one group discussion Simon and William articulated this necessity in physical terms.

'They [gay boys] wouldn't be too close,' William declared.

Simon nodded. 'Keep a distance.'

'Why keep the distance?' I asked.

They exchanged a glance and then Simon stated the obvious. 'Because other boys are going to think that you are also gay,' he told me patiently.

William began to add, 'Besides that – '

' – they would say you are in a relationship with him,' Thabiso cut in, at which the whole group dissolved into laughter.

Not only was the anxiety of being seen as 'gay' overwhelming for many of the adolescent boys, but 'gay' boys were also seens in some way as contagious. Herman articulated this: 'There is this other young boy who sometimes acts gay at school. When he turns to hug me or something, eish! I feel like a snake is going for my body. Because when I start thinking of myself acting as gay that thing makes me uncomfortable.' In Herman's case, at the thought of being hugged by a 'gay' boy, there was also a feeling of disgust. Many participants asserted that they were not comfortable forming close social relationships with 'gay' boys, fearing that if they were seen in their company, other boys might think they were gay too.

What was clear was that gay boys should be avoided at all costs because of a deep-seated fear of being contaminated by what some participants termed the 'disease of homosexuality', thereby resurrecting the outdated view that homosexuality constitutes an illness or mental disorder. My interviews with these adolescent boys revealed that claiming a 'gay' identity had powerful negative associations and any closeness with such an identity had to be strictly avoided, both literally and figuratively.

Some of the boys reported mixed feelings about befriending 'gay' boys. Simon, for example, disagreed with William, who in one of the focus groups expressed the strong opinion that all gay boys should be 'killed'. Drawing on a human rights perspective, Simon was of the belief that the rights of gay boys should be respected as they were also human beings, in a sense contradicting an earlier remark he had made that same-sex marriages should be opposed because they 'destroy families'. In response to William's radical opinion, Simon seemed to adopt a non-homophobic attitude towards gay boys: 'I respect them. It's not like I would look down on him when he passes by, or assault him.'

While these sentiments could still be viewed as prejudicial in that they reject only extreme homophobic behaviour, some attempts to engage positively with gay boys were evident. It is therefore important not to label all adolescent boys as homophobic.

A few boys demonstrated the emergence of (fragile) alternative non-homophobic voices, although they appeared to need external validation. For example, in one individual interview with me, Simon said that he did not have a problem befriending 'gay' boys at school provided they observed certain limits and restrictions. 'I don't mind to befriend "gay" boys,' he told me, 'as long as they don't propose love to me.' Simon's conflicting emotions when it came to befriending 'gay' boys came from a place of being worried about the possibility of being seen as a potential sexual conquest. If a 'gay' boy showed a sexual interest in him, he said, his first reaction would be cool rejection, but if the boy continued to pursue him, he might react violently.

'What would you do when he proposes love to you?' I asked him, at which he gave a thin smile.

'I would tell him politely that he must look at me well, as to who I am. I am not gay. I am not in that group, in that "family".'

'But if he pursues you?' I pressed.

'If he pursues me, obviously I would get angry because I am only human as well. Maybe to an extent of beating him up, but then as a guy he is going to fight back. It won't be like a male and female fight, but it's going to be a male to male fight.'

In the group interview, Simon tried hard to sound progressive, but many of his views were still implicitly homophobic. He supported his fellow group members in their view that 'gay' boys were seen as feminised, but asserted strongly that if a fight ensued between him and a gay boy, 'it won't be like a male and female fight, but it's going to be a male to male fight'. In putting it this way, Simon not only reinforced his own potency but also implied that being gay was a 'public performance', which might change if a gay boy was under siege to prove his maleness in a violent context, an idea that has also been observed in other research.[3]

Simon seemed to think that it would be an insult to his manhood for a gay boy to consider him an object of sexual desire, because he did not belong 'in that group [or] in that family', thereby positioning gay masculinity as 'other' and enabling him to distance himself from a gay identity. The possibility of being seen as a sexual object by another boy created anxiety in Simon, and, as a result, the more progressive, anti-homophobic views which he expressed in the individual interview changed radically in the focus group, where anti-gay sentiment was predominant. If he were to advocate gay rights, Simon might have feared he'd be seen as gay himself. Male bonding, according to Frosh and his colleagues, is often solidified and cemented among self-identified heterosexual boys in the kind of critical group conversation that was observed, and individual boys clearly did not want to be excluded from this kind of bonding.

Many of the boys in the individual interviews spoke about their fears and anxieties around being seen as gay due to their failure to live up to the image of township masculinity, which in many instances involved engaging in macho-type behaviours to prove one's manhood. The boys felt they did not have the freedom to choose their male friends because some boys had to be avoided due to their being gay or 'acting gay'. Most of the boys said that they knew gay boys at their school and that they felt uncomfortable around them. In one group interview, the boys told a story about a gay boy who flirted with other boys at school. Mpho began the conversations. 'It was that boy's party,' he said,

> and Martin and I did not know that he is gay. We went to the party and it was nice. The second day we noticed different moves and actions and the way he was talking that there is something wrong with this guy. So there were girls and boys and they exchanged numbers. He also had our numbers, and the next day I got a message that said Go outside; I will blow you a thousand kisses. I said to Herman I will not appreciate and I will not tolerate this thing. I said to Herman why don't you talk to this guy? Why is he doing this, sending us love messages? I said Herman, go and talk to this person. I do not know if Herman went and told him. K and I had that problem.

Everyone looked at Herman, who did not immediately volunteer a response.

'So, Herman, what is happening?' I prompted.

'Okay,' Herman said,

> in a way I was not a hundred per cent sure that he was gay. He is in the middle actually. When I confronted him, we decided, the three of us, Martin and Mpho, that we must confront him and ask him where he stands. If we say men and women, where would he stand?

Do you get my point? And then he actually got angry at me for asking him that question. That is why I am saying us straight guys do not hang around gays. They bring us down. At the end of the day, girls, when they see us hanging around with gays, they think that we are also gay whereby when I go to propose her, she says what are you doing, you are weak. You are gay!

The fear of being rejected by girls was another reason the boys gave for distancing themselves from 'gay' peers. They felt they needed to be consistent about their 'stand' in terms of their identity and preference for either men or women. The boy who was suspected of being gay was confronted and questioned about his sexuality because he apparently behaved strangely (walked and talked 'like a girl' and sent love messages to other boys). This behaviour was not in accordance with the boys' code, which stipulated that adolescent boys had to pursue and woo girls as potential sex partners. As in the case of Simon, who had earlier expressed anger at the prospect of being approached, Mpho was furious that the boy suspected of being gay had sent him a love message, and felt offended to be seen as the object of male desire. In the group interview, there was also a sense of feeling betrayed by this boy. As a result, the boy had to be confronted and compelled to declare whether he was straight or gay. In the participants' minds, it seemed impossible to be bisexual (you are either one of us or you are not).

In many respects, this group discussion was also about the constraints and boundaries placed on gay boys in terms of sexual expression and relationships with straight or other boys in general. 'Straight' boys evidently felt they had to avoid practices associated with femininity, such as hugging and sending other boys love messages, implying that adolescent boys cannot show affection to each other without provoking possible negative reactions. In this respect, it is worth noting that in talking about homosexuality, there was often a conflation between homosexuality as epitomised in feminised behaviour and attributes, and homosexuality as being about same-sex object choice.

In her study of adolescent boys, Cheri Pascoe observed that any boy who did something 'unmasculine' was likely to be called a 'fag'.[4] The 'fag' identity served as a disciplinary mechanism to ensure that all boys complied with the prevailing hegemonic norms of masculinity. Pascoe also found that the 'fag' slur was not limited to 'gay' boys but was employed in respect of any boy who temporarily failed to perform certain masculine activities in a given social space.

This captures some of the internal tensions, fears and anxieties that the adolescent boys in my study had to manage on a daily basis in order to maintain and sustain the image of being straight boys. In order to shore up their heterosexual identity, they had to very clearly and strongly *dis-identify* with homosexuality.

The boys also expressed discomfort with gay boys' tendency to spend most of their time with girls, despite the fact that they discriminated against gay boys at school. They saw same-sex relations as disruptive of existing gender relations as they felt that boys should spend time with other boys talking about sport (soccer, rugby and wrestling) and girls. They were very vocal about this in a group interview.

'They let us down because when they meet with girls they tell them our weak points,' said Peter with a slightly embarrassed grin, 'that guys are like this and that.'

Herman jumped in to agree. 'Just imagine I want a girl over there,' he said, pointing at the wall behind me. 'The next thing I go and talk to her – and maybe this gay guy does not like me and he goes to tell that girl that, ey, Herman is like this and this and this. In other words, as guys we are supposed to be united.'

Mpho nodded vehemently. 'They do, because they know much about girls because they always have a conversation with girls, and talk about boys, but he is a boy too. And then he emphasises that boys are wrong. And he forgets that he, himself, is a boy. And then that there are sorts of boys that we don't want ...'

In Peter noting feeling let down by gay boys and suspecting them of telling girls about boys' 'weak points', the implied suggestion was that girls might reject them as a consequence. Herman and Mpho also accused gay boys of not collectively protecting the interests of boys, of forgetting their gender. According to Herman, boys need to stand together in their mission to 'conquer' and 'play' girls, but gay boys evidently derailed such clandestine plans when they told girls that boys only wanted to have sex with them. The implicit accusation was that gay boys use their sexual orientation to get close to girls and to gossip about straight boys. In this group interview, gay boys were seen as 'sell-outs' or 'traitors' for telling girls male secrets.

There was an element of irony here, in that these boys expected some form of solidarity from a group of gay boys when most of their talk had constructed such boys as 'other' or had discriminated against them. Being gay and having close relationships with girls was seen as advantageous in a contradictory way because gay boys had unlimited access to girls. Beyond seeing such relations as threatening, the boys seemed envious of the closeness and openness of the relationships between gay boys and girls. Some of the boys jokingly talked about the need to pretend they were gay in order to access girls and spend time with them. At a deeper level, this demonstrated how the boys' conception of heterosexual masculinity constrained their desire for close relationships. Fear of being seen as gay also appeared to prevent boys from forming healthy non-sex-driven relationships with girls.

When I met him as a schoolboy Hilton openly self-identified as a gay boy but it soon became apparent that his had not been an easy emotional path. As he came to trust and relate to me he talked frankly about the challenges he faced in an environment like Alex. At school he came in for a lot of teasing and bullying over his sexuality, and at times struggled with depression, even feeling suicidal when it got intense. Teachers at his school were not especially supportive so he did not feel he could confide in anyone in a position of authority. Hilton took care over his appearance and was always stylishly dressed – he was brand-conscious and loved fashion – and he had a great sense of humour and charm.

In an individual interview, he refuted the accusation that he gossiped with girls about other boys. He said he spent a lot of time with girls because they did not discriminate against him. He also claimed that girls were less homophobic than boys, and that was another reason he enjoyed their company.

'I don't tell my [girl] friends what boys do,' he said. 'I don't tell them how and where boys change when they grow up. They talk about it in front of me, but I don't.'

'Do girls talk about girls' stuff with you?' I asked Hilton, at which his eyes sparkled with amusement.

'Yes,' he said.

'What do they tell you?'

'They will say, oh, my friend I'm on my periods. They will say, oh, these pads will break your virginity.'

'They say pads?'

'Yes, you know the ones that have a string.'

'Is it pads?'

Hilton frowned, as if I was being deliberately dumb. 'Yes, they have a string,' he insisted. 'They say it breaks their virginity.'

I was still puzzled. 'They do what?' I asked him.

'Break your virginity,' he said patiently. 'If you are still a virgin and you use those pads because you insert them they break your virginity. They talk about all these things in front of me, and I don't have a problem. They won't say this boy is not supposed to know girls' stuff. My friends are open and they just talk.'

That his girl friends could disclose this sort of information and talk about intimate female experiences such as menstruation supports the suggestion that girls feel a certain freedom in talking to gay boys. Pascoe believes that girls talk freely to gay boys because they are not seen as potential boyfriends and because they are friendly, less abusive and less violent.[5] It is possible that the 'straight' boys in my study were aware of the fact that 'gay' boys had access to intimate 'girls' stuff' and therefore in a sense had knowledge superior to their own.

They expressed the wish that they could have the same unrestricted contact with girls. As Simon put it, 'Girls always run away from us and like being with gay boys.'

Michael was of the view that gay boys spend a lot of time with girls out of fear of being rejected and out of wanting to align themselves with girls as a means of alleviating their anxiety about heterosexual relationships. 'From my personal point of view,' he said, 'I think boys who tend to change to being gay are insecure about themselves; they are afraid to be rejected by females. So they tend to act like females because they are afraid to go for females.' In this he was drawing on the stereotype that males may 'turn' gay because they have been hurt by females. He regarded himself as superior to the 'insecure' gay boys and as more confident and not afraid of rejection by girls. In being 'afraid to go for females', Michael was categorising gay boys as cowards.

All the 'straight' boys argued that gay boys should be denied masculine status for not complying with the norms of hegemonic masculinity, which include being sexually attracted to girls as well as accepting the challenge of possibly being rejected by them.

*

From our conversations during the interviews it became clear to me that boys police each other in subtle and less subtle ways in terms of boundaries, which is enforced through compulsory association with some boys (straight) rather than others (gay).

During the fieldwork stage of the project, some boys saw me giving Marcus a disposable camera. They immediately asked me why I had given him a camera because he was not a 'boy' but 'gay'. I asked them why they thought Marcus was gay, and they replied that he was gay because he spent most of his time with other gay boys at school. This, for me, was a clear indication of how the boys policed and discriminated against each other. Solely on the basis of his association with gay boys, Marcus was considered gay and, by implication, denied the identity of a 'real' boy. The boys suggested that Marcus should be excluded from a study on boys and masculinities because his masculinity was in doubt as he was not maintaining the strict boundaries between 'straight' and 'gay' boys. It seemed there was also an implicit fear that Marcus would contaminate their involvement in the research project or that his involvement would raise questions about their identities as straight boys.

The boys were adamant. They insisted that Marcus was not welcome to be part of the study. When I pushed them to elaborate on why they thought Marcus was gay, they told me he spoke 'like a girl'. One of the boys joked that Marcus's voice was too soft for him to be a boy. Boys should speak with a heavy accent and not with soft voices like girls. They mimicked how girls spoke, which led to a lot of laughter and agreement that boys had to avoid such behaviour at all costs.

Despite these accusations, I invited Marcus to be part of the research project. I wondered what the other boys thought about my 'transgression' in inviting a boy they considered to be gay to take part in the study. Did it raise questions for them about my sexuality (which is something I did not discuss with them)? In conducting interviews with lesbian schoolgirls, Pascoe found that her research participants were curious to know about her sexuality.[6] They wanted to know whether she was in a heterosexual or a homosexual relationship. It is possible that some boys may have wondered whether I was gay or straight, given my decision to include Marcus in the study.

In light of the other boys' accusations and homophobic comments, I was not comfortable including Marcus in the focus group, however. Only two individual interviews were conducted with Marcus at that time. Thereafter, from 2007 to 2017, I did 15 individual follow-up interviews with him. In the first individual interview in 2007, Marcus vehemently denied the rumour that he was gay. However, in 2009, during one of our individual follow-up interviews, he disclosed that he was gay.

He was indeed a soft-spoken young man, with a gentle manner and warm eyes. He wanted to be a hairdresser, which led to stereotypical assumptions on the part of those who were his peers at school and much derision and mockery.

Looking in some detail at the life stories of the two boys, Hilton and Marcus, who self-identified as gay in the study – Hilton from the outset and Marcus after some years – throws some interesting light on the lived experiences of black gay boys in the township of Alexandra. Their experiences and fear of homophobia confirm Deevia Bhana's contention that South African schools are homophobic due to teachers' negative attitudes to gay learners.[7] School learners who identify as gay find it hard to report experiences of homophobia at the hands of their peers to teachers, whom they consider to be homophobic as well. Some of these difficulties are highlighted in these two young men's stories, but the stories also show how they dealt with the homophobic experiences. They explain how they transitioned from being young adolescent 'gay' boys to young adults who became more confident and knowledgeable about their sexual orientation. During their young adulthood, they were more open and less apologetic about their sexual identities.

Hilton's story

During the fieldwork in 2007 Hilton was one of the boys who disclosed to me that he was gay. He was 15 years old at that time. He spoke about how other boys harassed him and called him derogatory names at school – 'They call me *isitabane*, faggot and say lots of other things.' Teachers did not do much to protect him, he said, as he had reported some of these abuses but nothing was done. This confirms Bhana's work about teachers' failure to deal with homophobia in schools. The abuses affected him emotionally, to the extent that he had even contemplated suicide. He spoke about his fears of living openly as a young adolescent gay boy at that time. As a result, he was confused, isolated and depressed and questioned his sexuality, feeling that it was wrong ('I hate being gay'). It is important to note that at that point Hilton was still young and in a phase of negotiating his identity; he felt uncertain about a lot of things as a gay boy and his knowledge about what it meant to be gay was limited.

This was illustrated in a first interview with me, when he articulated some of his fears and anxieties about sex in a gay relationship.

'Yeah, I ask myself the same question every day ... if you have sex – ' he gave a small laugh ' ... I can say yes.'

'What is it that you ask yourself?' I asked him.

Hilton laughed again and looked shyly at me. 'Who will penetrate who?' he replied, and then added, 'Do you understand?'

'Explain. Tell me more.'

'If we are dating, me and my boyfriend, it's obvious I'm the girl so he ...' His voice trailed away.

'He has to penetrate you,' I said.

'Yeah,' said Hilton. He gave another short laugh and looked down at his hands.

Hilton assumed that heteropatriarchal masculine stereotypes would also apply in gay relationships when it came to having sex,[8] modelling the stereotypical active/passive gender relations between heterosexual men and women. He thought that the gay man who occupied the position of the 'man' would decide when and how to have sex and assume the active, inserter role; the other man would take the passive, anal receptor role.[9] Passive partners tend to be feminised and are sometimes seen as inferior in the relationship.

However, the gay black men in Rankotha's study preferred 'flexible' role playing in bed, with partners taking turns to penetrate one another – this kind of pattern may be reasonably common.[10] Hilton was not sure if he wanted to take a passive or an active role but seemed to lean towards the former, seeing his identity as feminised. He was clearly worried about what his first sexual encounter would be like – whether it would be pleasurable or painful. He wanted to explore his fears but was not yet entirely relaxed when talking to me about sex, often laughing at my questions as a means of easing his nerves and fears. Interestingly, he did not complete his sentence when I asked him to tell me more about his fears and anxieties, reinforcing the idea that he was uncomfortable talking openly about the issue. I therefore completed his sentence with 'he has to penetrate you'. Eventually, he confided that he had been trying to find a partner but so far had struggled to meet someone as many boys were not yet out of the closet and identifying themselves openly as gay.

In the interviews, many of the boys were curious and voyeuristic about how gay males have sex and a number of them – Themba, for example ('I always ask myself how they do it. Is it not painful?') – associated sexual intercourse between gay men with pain. Some boys frowned when comments about gay sex were made, highlighting their feelings of disgust and repulsion and their sense that such sexual intercourse was aberrant. A common theme in all the group interviews was that gay boys were in some way letting straight boys down for not using their penises 'properly', that is, for penetrative vaginal sex. Gay boys were seen as deviating from the 'normal' sexual practice of 'screwing' and 'fucking' girls. In this narrative, gender and biology intersect. The dominant idea is that the penis should be used only for penetrative vaginal sex, with the implication that gay sex is not 'real' sex and that 'real' sex can only take the form of vaginal penetration. In this respect, there is little recognition that male homosexual sex might involve acts of penetration and be virile and active in expression. There is an assumed association between passivity and homosexuality.

Martin echoed other boys' sentiments that there was something wrong with gay boys' sexual desire. 'I normally ask myself about gays – is that as boys we feel – like maybe you meet a girl and you have feelings for her, and such things, you love her – and maybe she tempts you in such a way that ... like she touches you, and we boys are easily taken. But with a gay boy there is no magnet in him to get attracted to girls. He is just stiff.'

His main argument was that gay boys, in not having the 'magnet' to be sexually attracted to girls, remained frigid ('stiff') when girls touched them. His implication was that responding to a female's sexual invitation and having heterosexual desire are natural and inborn for any boy. He suspected that gay boys would not become aroused if girls tempted them (despite his ironic reference to 'stiffness') and would not get an erection in such a situation. He believed that there was a 'mismatch' between gay boys' biologically sexed bodies (possessing a penis) and their lack of sexual feelings for girls.

The assumption that sexed bodies and gendered identities are automatically intertwined is one that has been challenged by Judith Butler, who argues that there is no relation between sex organs, gender identity and desire and that we need to question the automatic association between these three elements.[11] The belief that, as articulated by Martin, boys should always be ready to have sex with girls makes an assumptive link between biology, desire and object availability. Martin's use of the pronoun 'we' to emphasise a sense of unity and sameness with other boys in the group interview suggests that this compulsion to perform straight masculinity is biologically, collectively and culturally imposed. In many of the group interviews, there was evidence of turn-taking to sustain a particular line of argument about gay boys' problematic lack of sexual desire for girls, which was seen as bizarre and strange.

'I can say that most of the boys are not interested in gays, because what they need from girls, gays do not have,' was how Alfred explained it.

'What is it that boys want from girls that gay boys do not have?' I asked, to which Alfred replied:

'I can say as a sexual healing – I can put it that way. Girls have different parts: titties and all that stuff. And gays do not have that; they just look exactly like mine.'

Alfred was explicit in his narrative that straight boys were not interested in 'gays' because they did not have 'titties and all that stuff', such as a vagina for 'sexual healing'. Many of the participants said that having vaginal sex and satisfying partners sexually was a priority in their relationships with girls. Alfred was puzzled as to how a boy could be sexually attracted to another boy because they both have the same sex organ (a penis). King was another boy who agreed with Alfred. 'I will never date a gay,' he proclaimed, 'because he has what I have. Why should I date him? He would not give me that much hundred per cent of what a girl would.' In other words, he would never date a gay boy because such a boy could not give him the vaginal sex and heterosexual interest and validation that a girl could. He also did not see any reason for dating a gay boy because 'he has penis and I also have penis'. Both Alfred and King implied that gay sex was necessarily lacking because it deviated from what they considered to be 'normal' – penetrative vaginal sex. Thus, it seemed that penetrative sex itself was not necessarily the issue but the *type* of penetrative sex. One wonders whether the boys would approve of anal sex between heterosexual partners and whether the issue was not essentially about object choice rather than practice. Alongside this strong 'biological' emphasis was a stereotypical and patriarchal understanding of sex, where vaginal penetration was more valued than any other form of sex, such as oral or anal. Using a penis 'properly' was equated only with penetrative vaginal sex.

Shaun was one of the boys who contended that being gay was something that could change and that sexual orientation was a malleable aspect of identity. In his individual interview, he spoke about his friend's gay cousin who was assaulted and forced to have sex with a girl. The cousin subsequently 'stopped being gay. He changed. Now you can say he is a player.' In a similar vein, sexual violence (especially rape) against lesbians is common in South African townships and is based on the belief that it will make lesbians heterosexual. Shaun's anecdote about his friend's cousin suggests that being gay was merely an act of performing the 'wrong' gender role.[12] He believed that gayness was something that could be 'cured' if a person was forcibly shown the 'right direction' and experienced heterosexual sex. Shaun implied that having sex with a girl was a good experience and that all gay boys needed to 'taste' it; they would then stop being gay and become casanovas ('players'). This discourse reiterates the idea that masculinity is not defined only in terms of heterosexual desire but also in terms of a male's ability to have sex with multiple partners – to be a 'player'.

The boys' negative reactions to homosexuality revealed the subtle power that gay masculinity has over hegemonic masculinity, contradicting the mainstream literature that epitomises gay masculinity as necessarily inferior.

Some boys spoke about the markers they used to determine whether a male was straight or gay. They asserted that they could tell if a boy was gay by the way he dressed.

'The first thing is they wear these [skinny trousers],' said King, laughing, 'and making themselves look sexy like girls.'

'Tight pants,' William agreed. 'Bum-shorts! You see them hugging and kissing. If you don't you will think they are girls and you can make a mistake of proposing – like Zenzo on *Generations*!' (The reference was to a scene in a popular television series in which two men kissed.)

King and William used existing social stereotypes to portray gay boys as flamboyant 'queens' who seek attention by wearing 'skinny trousers' and 'tight pants', but these comments also revealed something deeper. As straight boys, they appeared to see gay boys' dress style as a major threat to their sense of masculinity in that they – gay boys – turned themselves into objects of potential (male) sexual desire. William and King convey the kind of slippage that can take place if males, by virtue of their manner and dress, come to be mistaken for girls. Again, there seems to be some caricaturing of male homosexuality as necessarily involving the performance of a feminine identification and also an inadvertent acknowledgement that desire can be 'misplaced' and is therefore not as instinctive as the boys previously implied. It is possible that some of the participants may even have felt attracted to 'gay' boys who looked 'sexy like girls' by wearing tight pants. Pascoe found that many adolescent boys are privately sexually attracted to gay boys but that they repress these sexual desires because of the social stigma of homosexuality.[13] Psychoanalytically speaking, the degree of homophobia expressed could be understood as suggestive of a defensive position that implies the existence of repressed homoerotic desires and impulses.

Any such feelings or desires were denied by the participants when they depicted gay sex as repulsive and lacking in some way. The negative depiction of gay sex might have made the participants feel more masculine and less threatened by gay boys. However, their fears and anxieties did not disappear because they were confronted by gay images every day at school and in the media, such as on popular television programmes. They were thus aware of needing to engage with homosexuality, despite their generally rather conservative attitudes.

Hilton used his colourful clothing – in one of his photos he is proudly wearing a pink T-shirt – as a public marker to assert his gayness and to challenge the dominant norms of masculinity, which 'prohibit' adolescent boys from wearing certain clothes. Many straight boys at his school and in his township may have experienced his subversion of these boundaries as a threat to masculinity. He valued cleanliness, he said, and also loved taking care of himself. He positioned himself as superior to many 'dirty' straight boys. He was extremely critical of homophobic boys at his school. In his view they were immature and childish. He was no longer bothered, he said, by being called *isitabane*.

At the end of my interview with Hilton, he said, 'Some [boys] are hiding; when you look at them, they are straight and dress like other boys but they are gay on the inside ... So I don't care [about] people who discriminate against me ... This is who I am and [I] will not change because of them.' He emphasised that he was no longer bothered by other boys and their silly teasing behaviours. His suicidal feelings linked to being gay and the constant harassment he endured had dissipated.

Between 2007, when my research project began, and 2018 I had multiple follow-up interviews with Hilton. At the time of writing, he was 28 years old and living openly as a gay man, indicating a huge shift since our first two individual interviews when he was a schoolboy. Hilton has fully negotiated his identity as a gay man. He used some of our individual follow-up interviews to reflect on his high school experience and his frustration around the lack of information for young gay men growing up in townships.

I take that one back that I wanted to kill myself when I was still young,' he told me in one of our subsequent conversations. 'Eish, you can understand that I was young and confused. I did not [know] anything about being gay. I had to figure things [out] for myself. I'm now gay and happy about it. You know there is a lack of information for young gay boys so [they] end up being confused. It is frustrating. You go through everything all by yourself. I wish there can be information for other gay boys so that they don't go through the hell I went through. It was hell that, but I'm happy now. Yeah, being gay at that age it was not easy. It is not easy whereby you meet people who have stigma about your sexuality.

Hilton acknowledged that his journey from high school to his current life was not an easy path, but he felt relieved that he had not killed himself when I reminded him of our interview when he was 15 years old. He laughed with a sense of disbelief that he had wanted to end his life. 'It feels so good to be alive!' he exclaimed spontaneously. 'And as a gay man for that matter. I cannot trade being gay for anything. It is the best thing ever.' His strong view, however, is that support is needed for gay boys growing up in hostile homes or spaces characterised by homophobic attitudes. He acknowledged that he was lucky, however, in that his family had been supportive of his sexuality. They had not discriminated against him or treated him differently, but rather fully embraced his identity and supported him through his difficulties. He felt more knowledgeable about being a gay man now and confident about his sexuality. Previously, he had been in a steady relationship which lasted for four or five years before ending abruptly. We had a debriefing session about his feelings of hurt and disappointment around how the relationship ended.

At the time of writing in 2018, Hilton was in a new relationship and happy with how things were going, as well as with his life in general. He had accepted that a lot of people are still homophobic but this was no longer a personal cause for concern. He asserted with a big smile, 'Yes,

I'm gay, this is who I am, finish and *klaar*. I'm not going to apologise for being who I am. You either accept me or leave me alone.'

Hilton's long-held dream was to work as a stylist in the fashion industry and for this young man his dream was fulfilled. At the time of the interview, he had been working in the sector for eight years and he was employed by in a large retail store as a stylist. His plans were to move to the company's head office in Australia, thereby fulfilling another dream, that of getting international experience. He remembered our first interview while he was still in high school and talking that many years back about his ambitions to be a stylist, not to mention his preference for wearing the colour pink. He felt that he was living his dream to the fullest, including in respect of his taste for unique and colourful clothing. This was evident in some of the photos that he sent me between 2015 and 2018. Hilton said that he used fashion to disrupt stereotypes about gay men by also wearing clothes that were traditionally 'reserved' for and 'associated' with straight men. He alternated this with wearing very bright colours and tight pants that clearly 'show you that I'm gay and live with it'.

Being fashionable was a way to celebrate his identity as a gay man, although at times it increased his risk of being easily identifiable as such and thus subjected to homophobic abuse. In retrospect, he felt he was 'brave to wear pink clothes at that time [while still at school] because many people were highly homophobic ... and this is not they are currently not, but it is little bit better'. Hilton cynically raised a point that 'today it is more acceptable to see men wearing colourful clothes and justify that as colour blocking. I can say we are making some progress that people no longer associate pink with being gay.' His view was that the media played a positive role in promoting gay identities, giving the example of Somizi Mhlongo, a well-known black gay man and one of the judges on Idols South Africa. Hilton felt Mhlongo's presence on this popular television show put gay identity in a positive light through showing a successful gay man.

Despite his senior position at work and working for a company whose policy on matters such as non-discrimination was clear, Hilton still believes homophobia remains a problem and the struggle to fully liberate gay identities is a continuing one. He had colleagues, he said, who covertly harboured homophobic attitudes ('human behaviour is human behaviour'; 'anti-discrimination policies alone are not enough').

Looking back to his own experience in navigating his sexuality from boyhood to manhood, he recommended providing support to gay boys in high schools and putting strategies in place to protect them in that environment. Furthermore, he maintained, interventions were also needed for school teachers to deal with their own homophobic attitudes, something that could also be extended into the workplace.

Marcus's story

Marcus was the participant whom the other boys in the study asserted should not be part of the project because he was supposedly gay. This was mainly based on the fact that he had a soft voice and appeared too soft physically to be a 'real' boy. In the first interview I had with him, Marcus mentioned that he wanted to be a hairdresser when he grew up but denied the allegation that he was gay. I picked up on his professional ambitions.

'Does this say anything about your identity?' I asked him.

'Yes,' Marcus told me. 'People would think that he is a hairdresser, he is gay or something. They do not understand that in life you need to have a career that you will follow.'

'And you say it also says something, partly; it is not that it's because of your identity. When I was asking you about who you are and all that, you did not say anything about your identity as a gay boy?'

'No, I am not gay,' he said quietly. 'I am Marcus, a person who likes people, and I am bright.'

'I mean, when you are a hairdresser people automatically think you are gay.'

'Most people think that you have chosen to be a hairdresser, and most hairdressers are gay.'

'And you say you are not?'

'I am not,' said Marcus.

I need to acknowledge that I went into this interview with the agenda of wanting to find out whether Marcus was gay or not because of what the other boys had told me earlier. My questions here reveal that I explicitly pushed Marcus to say something about his sexual identity. With hindsight and self-reflection, I was able to uncover my own prejudices in associating certain occupations (in this case hairdressing) with being gay.

From a young age Marcus was fascinated by the skill that went into cutting hair. Later he would tell me that he'd watch closely when a barber was plying his trade, taking note of the pride that went into a good job and seeing how this would bring joy to the barber's customers.

Marcus denied being gay, but said he knew that the other boys at school thought he was. He added that it did not concern him unduly because he knew he was not. Marcus was confident in talking about his identity and masculinity (also disclosing that he was proud to be a virgin), and in rejecting risk-taking behaviours associated with being a 'real' township boy in Alex. It is possible that other boys might have accused Marcus of being gay because he did not comply with the 'unwritten rules' of hegemonic masculinity, such as displaying aggression, spending time with other boys, playing football and dating multiple girlfriends. Marcus was thus perhaps being punished for not conforming to the gender expectations of compulsory hegemonic masculinity. In the context of Alexandra, his lack of conformity led to him being categorised as 'other'.

In our second individual follow-up interview, Marcus told me that he had a girlfriend whom he'd met a few days after our first interview. This disclosure was interesting for a number of reasons. I wondered whether Marcus told me about his new girlfriend as an explicit marker of a heterosexual identity and as a face-saving strategy to demonstrate that he was straight. He might also have made the disclosure in an attempt to consolidate his sense of masculinity by playing the 'macho' role in the follow-up interview. Surprisingly, in this interview, Marcus said that he was planning to have sex with his new girlfriend soon but that he would respect her decision if she said she was not ready. Two points warrant further analysis. On the one hand, Marcus embraced an alternative voice that was non-coercive towards his girlfriend – he accepted that no meant no. However, on the other hand, Marcus experienced some internal conflict about the fact that he had never had sex. He felt pressurised that the time had come for him to be sexually active. Again, I wondered if Marcus's sudden decision to be sexually active was perhaps the result of pressure to prove to his peers (and to me) that he was not gay but straight. In his reflections on the research project, Marcus said, 'I wish it was possible to continue and continue with this so that we as boys can continue talking about our feelings.' For the whole of 2007, Marcus denied that he was gay.

In 2009, Marcus called me to say he wanted to discuss something with me. He said he had been self-reflecting since our last meetings in 2007 and 2008. We arranged to meet and when we did Marcus disclosed to me that he was gay. He also wanted to explain his earlier denial. At that time, he said, despite knowing that he was not like other boys in his neighbourhood, he was unsure and still confused about his identity. He said he was happy being a 'gay' boy, however, and his family had accepted him when he came out to them. Both his parents were supportive, especially his mother.

At the time of completing this book, Marcus was 28 years old and working as a hairstylist in a salon in Sandton, Johannesburg, after completing a diploma in Cosmetology at the College of Johannesburg and spending years of apprenticeship and perfecting his craft. He learned as much as he possibly could, not only the creative stylist side but also about products, different hair qualities and how to get the best results for clients. He kept abreast of hair fashion and identified specialist practitioners from whom he could learn more. He progressed steadily, working in different salons and gaining a reputation for excellence.

He felt liberated that he had come out about his sexuality and he was happy to be living openly as a gay man. He acknowledged that our follow-up interviews had made him feel safe enough to reflect on himself and that the environment we'd created in that space had built his confidence to come out. And he loved his job as a hairstylist (figure 10 shows some of his work as a hairdresser).

Figure 10: Satisfied clients – some photos showing Marcus's hairstyling flair.

'I can say I'm living my dream,' he said, smiling broadly as we drank our coffee. 'It was in 2007 when I told you I want to be a hairdresser and we laughed about it. Now here I'm working at the salon and making hairs and nails of famous people of TV. I was involved in the make-up of models for bridal magazines and other glossies and many other important events, including Mercedes Benz Fashion Week. Yes, it is me rubbing shoulders with who's who of South Africa and people that many of you see on TV. I can make their hair and nails.'

In total, since our first interview in 2007, Marcus and I had 18 interviews. His main narrative was that of success of a black gay man who grew up in Alexandra township. He was highly appreciative of our follow-up interviews, claiming that they had helped him gain some insight about himself and tensions associated with being a gay man. In some of the interviews, Marcus also spoke about 'straight' men who have sexual relationships with 'gay' men. He noted that some of those men were married to women and were thus living a double life. He felt liberated that he did not need to live a lie and could express his sexuality without fear of being judged. His view was that people need to come out of the closet and live their lives freely. He spoke openly about his sexual practices, including whether he was 'a top or a bottom' (he described himself as a bottom). He was in a steady relationship, he confided, but his partner was shy about the fact that they lived openly as a gay couple, resulting in the relationship being 'on and off'. The fact that his partner was not yet fully committed to their relationship was a cause of some frustration for him. His personal long-term plan was to have children, either through adoption or a surrogate mother.

Marcus remains the soft-spoken, humble and down to earth person he was growing up to be when he and I first met. He has always believed in the value of working hard and, together with his entrepreneurial spirit, networking, and his creative flair, professionally he appears to be well on his way to his long-term goal of owning his own salon. He has continued to forge ahead in his chosen profession, adding being the official hairstylist to beauty pageant contestants to his list of accomplishments and being interviewed in magazines as a celebrity hairstylist to the stars.

8 | Young Fathers and the World of Work

Many of the adolescent boys in the study did not know their fathers and had grown up with little or no contact with them. The effect this had on their lives was a prevailing theme. In the interviews, they spoke about wanting to be 'different' fathers compared to their absent fathers and expressed the wish to be good role models to their children when they became parents one day. What was progressive was that the emphasis in their narratives about fatherhood was not only on fathers meeting the physical needs of their children, but meeting their emotional needs as well. It was evident that the boys had created an 'ideal' picture of themselves as wanting to be good fathers in the future.

During the fieldwork stage in 2009, three of the boys became fathers and so the interviews I conducted with these young men were also used to discuss how they experienced this.

Considerable research has been done on teenage pregnancy in South Africa,[1] but most of it has focused only on teenage mothers. However, because of the circumstances that arose and the opportunity that presented itself to me, I was able to contribute to work that had already done in the field of reseach on teenage fathers by Sharlene Swartz and Arvin Bhana, as well as Robert Morrell, Deevia Bhana, Tamara Shefer and their colleagues.[2] I was able to reflect the voices of Oupa, Timothy and Nelson, whose girlfriends became pregnant that year; in addition, as mine was a longitudinal study, I was also able to describe the experiences of some of the boys who became fathers later, when they were young adults.

Three adolescent boys, Oupa, Timothy and Nelson, while talking about their absent fathers (Chapter 4), also spoke about their own experiences of becoming teenage fathers. All three teenage fathers were actively involved in their children's lives, thus contradicting the dominant view that teenage fathers very seldom accept responsibility for supporting their children. None of the pregnancies were planned and the boys were shocked when they received the news from their respective girlfriends.

'What was your first reaction?' I asked Oupa.

'I became scared,' he said, 'and I told her I will see. I will just have to tell my old lady [his mother] and I don't know how she's going to react.'

Timothy didn't want to believe the news. 'When she first told me, I thought she was joking. When time passed I started seeing changes and I asked her if she was serious.'

'Were you not scared?' I asked him, although I could see the answer on his face.

'I was scared,' he said.

Nelson only told his mother that his girlfriend was pregnant with his child six months after she'd broken the news to him, but he had an excuse. 'My girlfriend's family did not come to report at my place. Like you know culturally they are supposed to come and report that your child has impregnated our daughter and stuff. They did not come.'

Not only were the boys scared and shocked at this unanticipated event but they also worried about how their mothers would react to the news that their girlfriends were pregnant. All three stated that they did not immediately tell their parents due to their fear of being shouted at. They said this was a very stressful period for them.

When I met him at the beginning of our project Oupa described himself as a *tsotsi* boy and a *sex-jaro*. He was not over concerned about his grades as a school learner and was proud of the fact that he had multiple girlfriends. The news of the pregnancy took him completely by surprise. He was not a boy given to discussing feelings and emotions, but he became depressed when the reality of his changed status began to sink in and some of the sessions he and I held were debriefing ones.

'The stress was killing me,' he admitted in an interview. 'I was even thinking maybe I have bad luck or something.' He had not expected his girlfriend to fall pregnant – 'I used to think only older people go through this thing [making someone pregnant]'. Oupa wished he could go back and undo the whole thing and he was full of remorse. He added that he had not had enough information about sex at the time and that the workshops he attended did not give him sufficient information on teenage pregnancy to have anticipated this outcome.

Both Oupa and Timothy said that it took them three to four months before they told their parents about their girlfriend's pregnancy. The reason for Nelson's reticence, as he explained, was culturally based.

Culturally, in this situation, it is customary for the girl's family to go to the boy's family to report the matter once they discover that their daughter is pregnant. In return, the boy's family has to pay 'isisu or inhlawulo' (damage money for impregnating a girl out of wedlock) if their son accepts paternity.[3] In the past, paying damages involved handing over livestock, but today paying damages involves the exchange of money. For most families, the amount ranges between R5 000 and R10 000, but this differs from one family to another and some families may demand more.[4] Interestingly, the three teenage fathers in this study were not requested to pay isisu or inhlawulo. It seems this practice is not common in urban contexts such as Alexandra, possibly due to the erosion of cultural practices in the townships or the lack of fathers and close male relatives, such as uncles, to negotiate the damage money. In their study, Swartz and Bhana found that paying isisu or inhlawulo was at times an impediment to fatherhood because many boys and young men refused to acknowledge paternity and deserted their children owing to their inability to afford this 'damage' payment.[5] Some researchers, such as Dorrit Posel and Stephanie Rudwick, argue that paying isisu or inhlawulo is slowly losing its cultural significance as a symbol of apology to a girl's family because of the high cost of the damages.[6]

The three teenage fathers in this study did not deny their paternity. It was not clear, however, whether they accepted this in part because their girlfriends' families had not approached their families to demand they pay *inhlawulo* and therefore they had not had to negotiate the affordability of acknowledging paternity. Nelson, who was 17 years old at the time, said that he would have acknowledged paternity in any case despite his peers advising him to deny paternity when he told them his girlfriend was pregnant. He vehemently rejected their advice, saying he could not disown his own 'blood'. His argument was that refusing to acknowledge his own blood would bring bad luck and possibly anger from the ancestors. After his child was born, *mopaso wa go bega ngwana* (a cultural ritual to introduce the child to the ancestors) took place. He believed that the birth of a child was a gift that had to be celebrated, even though this child had not been planned. His newly born baby boy was central in his life. Unlike his absent father, he wanted to be there for his child and take good care of him. He said boldly in the interview: 'I want my child to experience my love as the father and not experience the pain I had of growing without my father. I don't want my child to suffer the pain I suffered.'

By being an involved father, Nelson seemed to be vicariously fulfilling some of his unmet emotional needs as a boy child himself of growing up without his father. The interview revealed that the birth of his child had reactivated some of his unresolved childhood issues with regard to his absent father. In the interview, he vacillated between two positions, of talking about his absent father as a bad father and himself as a good father figure because of his caring and active involvement in his child's life. He emphasised the view that men should never abandon their children as this leaves the children with so much pain. He was pleased, he said, to have the opportunity of the interview to talk about his pain and reflect about his new status as a teenage father. He added that he had never expected the interview to elicit so many strong feelings in him.

Oupa and Timothy also spoke about wanting to be 'good' fathers, in contrast to their own absent fathers, suggesting that in becoming fathers their own experiences of being fathered were evoked, probably both consciously and unconsciously. They both said they felt committed to their new roles as teenage fathers and confirmed that they were actively involved in their children's lives.

Oupa was struggling to make sense of things, and he started smoking and drinking heavily at this time to try and forget about his problems. He was especially worried, still being at school and trying to cope with day-to-day schoolwork, about not being in a position to support his newborn daughter financially.

'Sometimes she gets sick and you find that I have stress because I was at the clinic the whole night and I can't go to school the following day. Those are the things that were stressing me. Sometimes I want to do something for her and then the next thing she's sick and I'm at the clinic and then I can't do my schoolwork; I fall asleep in class ...'

His son's health was also a preoccupation for the level-headed Timothy, who still lived with his parents. 'I worry when he's sick or has a rash and think what if something happens to him,' he admitted.

'When he's not feeling well, do you become stressed?' I asked.

Timothy nodded, frowning and running a hand over his head. 'It happens sometimes when he's sick that his mother doesn't tell me and it's one of the things that stresses me because she waits for me to ask her what's going on with the baby.'

It was clear that the emotional costs of being teenage fathers were high. Oupa's daughter had some worrying health issues soon after she was born, which lasted nearly three months, much of which time she spent in hospital. 'I had to be supportive to the mother [his girlfriend],' 17-year-old Oupa told me. 'I didn't want her to feel like she had the baby alone. We did this together.' His admission indicated that he was willing to take on the responsibility of supporting his girlfriend emotionally. He did not want her to feel alone in looking after their sickly child, whom he recognised as their joint responsibility. Oupa was also proud about taking on the conventionally female role of feeding his daughter and changing her nappies. He argued that as a teenage father he needed to do all these 'feminine' chores in order to bond with his child. Both Oupa's and Timothy's views signified that as teenage fathers they were slowly embracing the voices of responsible fatherhood characterised by emotional care, love and concern. Despite their youth, they appeared to have adopted responsive and responsible roles in relation to their children and to have been willing to demonstrate 'new father' attributes.

However, the interviews also revealed that teenage parenthood took its toll on teenage fathers and mothers, particularly in terms of academic performance. All three boys said their academic performance declined after their girlfriends got pregnant and also after the girls had given birth. Oupa and Timothy were repeating grades 11 and 12, respectively, at the time of the interviews, and attributed their academic failure to stressors associated with being teenage fathers. For example, Oupa reported that he and his girlfriend missed classes to take their baby to the hospital. He found it difficult initially to adjust to his new role and his drinking and smoking became excessive; with time he realised that this behaviour was not helping him. 'I did not want to be like the old man [his absent father],' Oupa explained, and so he stopped his heavy drinking and smoking. He was determined to offer his child a 'different' experience of growing up, one that was an improvement on his own father-related experiences.

'I want to do things for my child so she can have a better life than I did and guide her not to experience the things that I did,' he said.

Nelson's recollections of his father not being part of his life were similar, as was his determination to be a different kind of dad for his son.

'It is painful growing up not knowing your father,' he said. 'I really want to be a different father.'

'And do you think you would be free to talk to him?' I asked, meaning his son.

Nelson nodded vehemently. 'Yes,' he said. 'Because I do not want him to do the mistakes I did.'

Oupa, Timothy and Nelson all demonstrated that they were emotionally invested in being caring and non-destructive fathers. In many of the ways they expressed this, a significant part of being a 'good' teenage father was about rectifying their own absent fathers' mistakes as far as possible in their own relationships with their babies and the babies' mothers. Nelson was adamant that he would talk more openly to his son about issues of sex and teenage pregnancy to ensure that he did not make the same mistake as he'd done of impregnating a girl at a young age. He believed he would not have made this mistake if he had had a male figure in his life to guide him in this respect.

It was very clear that the teenage fathers did not want their children to experience the pain they had endured. Perhaps aware of the irony, given his self-identified *sex-jaro* status at school, Oupa said that he would be overprotective of his daughter to ensure that boys did not 'play games' with her (meaning cheat on her or treat her as a sex object). It was interesting that he could now appreciate that this was a risk. He would be sure to teach his daughter when she was older to be careful of boys and their lies, he said.

Although at the time of the particular interview in which he asserted this Oupa was separated from his girlfriend (the mother of his daughter, who by then was three years old), he told me that he made sure that he saw his daughter almost every day. 'I do not want her [his daughter] to be like me. My father stays in Orange Farm and I'm staying with my mother here in Alexandra. I see him [his father] once in a while. He does not visit us. So I don't want my daughter to experience that.' Unlike his absent father, Oupa was happy to spend time with his daughter.

The other two teenage fathers also spoke about the importance of fathers spending time with their children. Although the emphasis was on meeting the emotional and physical needs of their children, they were frustrated by their inability to meet their material needs. In this respect, they believed they were not good enough as fathers because they did not have money to support their children and had to rely on their parents (especially their mothers) for their own and their children's financial support.

In their study on teenage fatherhood in South Africa, Swartz and Bhana also found that teenage fathers battled with some of these issues.[7]

Another major struggle was managing the tensions of being a teenager and a father at the same time. The narratives that emerged in my study supported this; they revealed a sense of feeling forced to grow up too quickly and pressure to stop behaving like 'typical' teenage boys.

'I can't enjoy it [being a teenager] any more since having a child, eish, it's difficult,' said Oupa. 'Everything I do I must do to please her because I brought her into the world and not to make her suffer.'

Timothy missed a teenager's spontaneity or impulsiveness. 'I can't just do things without thinking first,' he said. 'Now when I have money I can't just go and spend it. I have to think about the child. I feel different.'

Both Timothy and Oupa acknowledged that having a child was a big challenge and that they needed to be more responsible in their behaviour. Oupa said that he used to smoke a lot of dagga (marijuana), but now that he had a child 'you can't be buying dagga all the time when your child needs certain things'. As a teenage father, whatever he did, he first had to think about his daughter. At the time of the interview, Oupa was selling sweets and cigarettes at school and, with the little money he earned, he was able to buy a few things for his daughter. He interpreted this as being responsible and making compromises ('not buying dagga') to ensure that his daughter did not 'suffer'. He wanted his daughter to live a better life because he had 'brought her into this world', indicating his sense of both burden and responsibility. Oupa was very appreciative that his mother supported him as well as his daughter. He wanted 'to see her [his daughter] in school and me being able to take her to school in my car, living in my house and me being able to give her money, my money not my mother's money'. He regretted getting his girlfriend pregnant but claimed that the experience had taught him a valuable lesson. He felt he had 'grown' as a result and was more mature than his male peers. As a teenage father, he told his peers 'that having a child is not easy' and advised them about reducing their risk in relation to both unplanned pregnancy and contracting HIV/AIDS. He also began to focus more on his schoolwork. He wanted to complete his matric and study chemical engineering at university. In another follow-up individual interview,

Oupa said he had found a piece job at a local supermarket after school hours. He was grateful that he could now support his daughter with his own money and did not need to rely on his mother's money.

Tragically, Oupa was shot and killed on his way back from work one evening. He was allegedly caught in the crossfire when two men started fighting over a girl in a local tavern in Alex. The perpetrator was not arrested due to lack of evidence. His mother was devastated by his death. I, too, was devastated, particularly because in our individual follow-up interview, Oupa had sounded so positive about the future. He had said that the experience of being a teenage father had taught him many lessons about life and that he had decided to create a new life for himself and to be more responsible in his behaviour.

These three teenage fathers' narratives all clearly showed that the stress of being fathers at such a young age served as a trigger for personal growth and positive change in their lives. Like Oupa, 17-year-old Timothy also believed he had 'grown' as a result of his experience of becoming a teenage father. He reported that his character had changed and that he was more responsible. He was the boy who had previously boasted that he had more than eight girlfriends and that he had had sex with all of them. After his baby boy was born, however, he stopped doing a lot of things, such as 'having many girlfriends', as he described it. Unlike Oupa, who had separated from his girlfriend, Timothy was still in a relationship with the mother of his son. She was doing Grade 11 at the time of the interview. For Timothy, the meaning of his son's name, Lesedi (Tswana word for light), was significant for him. His son had become his 'light' and he, himself, was now able 'to see the light'. Consequently, he now avoided risk-taking behaviours such as drinking excessively or having sex with multiple partners. In our follow-up interview, he spoke about the importance of being loyal and faithful to the mother of his child. His main goal was also to complete his matric and to study for a Bachelor of Commerce degree at the University of Johannesburg. He did complete his matric but was not able to go to university due to lack of finances.

Overall, the participants felt triumphant that they had managed to deal with many of the challenges of teenage fatherhood. Despite anxieties and pressures, this experience transformed their sense of self. The positive changes that followed included making sacrifices in their personal lives, such as not spending money on alcohol, dagga or expensive brand-name clothes; becoming monogamous; and seeking part-time employment so that they could support their children. The participants evidently had the capacity to reflect on what the birth of their children had meant for them, their identities and their future. The period before (and in some cases immediately after) their girlfriends falling pregnant was in some instances characterised by self-destructive risk-taking behaviours, but later they felt they had to become more reflective about their behaviours. The boys believed they had experienced personal growth, which helped them to reorganise their goals and ambitions in life, including completing their schooling, undertaking tertiary studies and finding better jobs to support their children. All three boys appeared to have developed a greater sense of purpose in life. It would be interesting to explore the long-term sustainability of these positive feelings they had about themselves and their plans for the future. That said, the participants might well have used the notion of personal growth to deny negative feelings associated with teenage fatherhood, although it is recognised that personal growth following a stress-related event is possible and may be important in mobilising the inner resources for healing and for positive change. It should be noted, however, that such growth is not only a personal experience – it is also facilitated by other factors, such as social support, and this may have been a crucial element in the lives of these particular boys. Social support provided by parents, especially mothers, seemed to play a central role in this process of positive change. The study showed that the participants' mothers, now also grandmothers, supported their grandchildren and encouraged their sons to be 'good' fathers. These mothers provided emotional support to their sons in coping with the new responsibilities of being teenage fathers and helped them to manage their related stress and anxiety. This is in line with Jay Fagan and Elisa Bernd's finding that the support of family members has a positive influence on teenage fathers' involvement in their children's lives.[8] In this respect, my study's findings regarding teenage paternity, although based on a very small population of three, suggest that boys may be more willing to shoulder responsibility in this regard than is generally expected or thought to be the case.

*

At the time of completing this book in 2019, six other participants in my study had children. I had first met them when they were schoolboys and now they were all between the age of 25 and 28. I had betweeen 10 to 19 follow-up interviews with them. Two were married, three were living with the mothers of their children and one was separated from the mother of his child. Their experiences of being married, in steady relationships and being fathers were discussed in the follow-up interviews. As with Oupa, Timothy and Nelson, who became fathers in their teens, these young men's narratives, too, revealed how their own fathers' absence played a role in their wanting to be 'good' fathers themselves. The negative comparison to their own absent fathers was a common theme.

Martin's story

At the time of completing this book, Martin was 27 years old. I met him when he was 15 and in Grade 10. He went on to complete his matric and after school he went to Boston College but was not able to complete his studies due to lack of finances. He then completed a certificate in Information Technology in 2011. This certificate training was provided free of charge to unemployed young people. He was able to find temporary jobs but described this period of his life as difficult as none of the jobs paid well. In 2012, he was recruited into a learnership programme at a well-known company, and was later hired permanently. He had been working for that company ever since. He met his partner in 2012 and they got married in 2015. They live together in a suburb in the south of Johannesburg so Martin has moved out of Alex, which for him epitomises success. He asserted that his life story showed 'that the hood [slang word for township] is not a determining factor of who you become in the future. You need to know what you want in life and persevere. I persevered.'

Even as a schoolboy, Martin had been clear about his career goals and his determination to make something of himself. He was a reserved boy but became more talkative as time went on. Close to his mother, he, like many of the other boys, had felt the absence of a father keenly. He told me he had found our interview sessions extremely valuable, particularly in terms of his emotional growth. 'I must say those conversations about being a man did help because after our meetings with you we started meeting on our own and talking about the question of manhood and what it means to be a boy in Alexandra.'

After completing his matric Martin and his friends went further, beyond the research project. They joined a men's dialogue forum in collaboration with Brothers for Life to encourage young boys and men in Alex to talk about masculinities, drug abuse and violence. Martin reflected that so much insight was gained out of these conversations, including my interviews with him. He felt his identity as a young black man was shaped by all these conversations.

In one of our follow-up interviews, he spoke about his elation when he learned that his wife was pregnant. 'From the moment we knew about the pregnancy,' he told me, smiling, 'we went together to the gynaecologist, went for check-ups. And everything is fine.'

This sort of step – accompanying a partner to an appointment with a gynaecologist – may represent a more general shift in young men's attitudes. Some of the other participants in the study confirmed that they, too, were willing or wanted to assist their partners in parenting, including going with them for hospital check-ups. This eagerness to support their female partners emotionally, perhaps indicates a shift – that they no longer see motherhood or being pregnant as the sole burden of the female partner. Martin felt it was their joint responsibility and did not want his pregnant wife to feel that she was alone. He wanted to 'enjoy each step of the pregnancy' and was excited to be at the birth of his son. He also saw it as going some way to healing the family after tragedy.

> It's nice because I think it's every man's dream to have a first born as a boy. Yes. That was my wish, and God answered my prayers and gave me a boy. And I was so happy. It means what I wished for came to pass. After my brother lost a son in 2013, we were scared to have children – thinking what if I have a child and then something like that happened in future. And then the blessing that she will give birth to is the one that will fill up the space. Not that it will close the space, but it will bring about healing – and the family will grow.

Martin was extremely happy to be a father. His child was regarded as a blessing for the family after his brother had lost a son. Despite his excitement, he was also anxious about being a father, especially because he had not had a positive male figure in his life. However, he was confident that he would manage and learn as he went along. For him, being a father meant being a 'supplier of caring, and supplier of love to your family and those you have around you. That is what it means to me about being a father. You are simply three words: family, love and caring.' Care and love were at the centre of what Martin regarded as being a good father, contrary to the traditional conception of fathers being the providers or breadwinners. This is not to suggest he did not say anything about that role, but he repeated the importance of love and care as key attributes of being a good father. He also emphasised the role of the environment in which a child grows up, which he felt should be characterised by a loving relationship between parents.

> I'm very close to my wife. We are very, very close. It is close that we talk about many things. Love depends on communication. If you and your partner understand each other, and talk

about things – even if there is misunderstanding – you'd reach agreements. You are able to make sacrifices. Many people limit love to feelings and emotions, but it is not just about that. It's about how you and your partner reach common agreements even if you have differences. That is what I believe. I do love her, and she is a person I want to spend my life with.

Martin and his partner's closeness was evident when their baby boy got so sick that he had to be hospitalised for four months. During this period, Martin experienced high levels of stress but felt that he needed to be emotionally strong for his wife. They went to the hospital to visit the child almost every day. Very sadly, the child's health deteriorated after an operation and he passed away. Martin and his partner were devastated. He spoke to me at length about his loss and both he and his partner attended grief counselling. I continued to provide Martin with emotional support during that period. He reflected deeply about his loss and asserted that it was important for men to talk about their feelings. He found counselling helpful in assisting him to process his loss. Slowly, Martin began to function better, claiming in a later interview that he was 'feeling my old self again though I still think of my son. I still miss him but I'm okay'. He spoke about the need to create awareness campaigns to assist men to talk openly about their feelings. He felt that this would also help to reduce violence against women, which he believed was often due to 'an anger that we men have for not talking about our problems'. He wanted to start a non-governmental organisation to assist men but did not manage to get it off the ground due to work commitments. His view about life was positive again, which was a sign that he had managed to process the loss of his son. When Martin called me mid-year in 2017 to say his wife was pregnant again, I was overjoyed. Martin was excited but also extremely anxious, given his previous loss. His wife subsequently gave birth to a baby girl, to whom Martin is devoted.

When we met for an interview over coffee Martin once again shared some of his reflections with me on growing up in Alex and growing up without a father. People often used their upbringing as an excuse for their failures in life, he said, but he refused to buy into that idea. He would not allow his upbringing or circumstances to define him as a person. 'I worked hard to achieve my goals,' he said. 'It is all about hard work.'

In another of our interviews he gave the example of his older brother who had wanted to be a lawyer, but who did not become one because, after completing matric, he started hanging out with bad friends who smoked and drank heavily. He had confronted his brother about this.

'Today I look at him, I said look at yourself, I feel I should give you a mirror and look at yourself. And then I would rephrase the questions and you answer. Firstly, you wanted to become a law student, to be a lawyer for the future. Look at the mirror and tell me if it is reflecting what you wanted before, or is it something different? What went wrong actually? He couldn't answer.'

Martin's view was that his brother's situation could not be blamed purely on his circumstances, which he considered an excuse. Rather, he felt that the choices we make as youngsters catch up with us later in life.

Following the birth of his daughter, he said, 'Life is great for now. It has its own challenges, but we can handle the challenges.' He was looking forward to raising and to having more children in the future.

His daughter was almost two years old when I completed this book and Martin's face lit up when he talked about her. She was growing very fast, he said, and becoming a 'big girl'. His wish for her was that she would grow up in a world free of violence against women. He remained passionate about community work and still hoped to form an NGO that could help young boys and men to self-reflect and think positively about their masculine identities. In the meantime he assists in various community projects, including one that helps orphaned children.

Herman's story

Herman was 14 years old when we met for our first interview in 2007 and 28 at the time of completing this book. He was regularly teased by *tsotsi* boys for being a fool because of his studious behaviour when he was still in high school. In total, we had 13 individual follow-up interviews between 2007 and 2018.

At the time of writing, Herman was working for a private company as a financial administrator. In addition to this work, he also provided tutorial classes in commercial subjects (accounting, auditing, business management) to matric learners and university students in and around Alex. Providing these classes, he said, was his way of putting back into his community to encourage young people to be more committed to their schoolwork. His view, echoing Nelson Mandela's words, was that 'it is only through education that a child of a working-class parent can be something in life'. His long-term plan was to run these tutorial classes on a full-time basis and he was busy talking to private companies and the Department of Education in an effort to persuade them to buy into his initiative to provide extra support to school-going learners after school hours and on weekends. He saw this as a practical way in which to improve the quality of high school education in South Africa, adding that programmes such as these should be linked to financial assistance for learners who passed matric so that they could access institutions of higher learning.

Herman also reflected about his own experiences of schooling in Alexandra. He mentioned that no detailed career guidance had been provided at his school and that he was stranded after passing matric as he had not applied to any university. He added that finances were also a major stumbling block in terms of going to university. However, one of his teachers called him to tell him about a bursary that was available, which he then applied for and got. He registered at the university to study for a Bachelor of Commerce degree. His university experience was not pleasant, however, as the bursary only covered half of his fees and no other expenses. As a result, he had to find the transport money to travel daily to campus from Alexandra and there were days when he was not able to attend lectures because he could not get the money simply to get there. He also had to raise extra money every year for registration to cover the shortfall. His view in one of our follow-up interviews was that the #FeesMustFall movement was raising real issues that affect poor black students in universities.

'As a black student,' Herman said, with the rueful, heartfelt conviction of one who had been there, 'you are not only stressing about your schoolwork like white kids or rich children. You stress about money for transport. You stress about accommodation and food. You stress about so many things but you are still expected to pass no matter what. It is an unfair system that you are just stressing.'

Despite these difficulties, Herman managed to complete his university studies and was motivated to develop his academic support programme for school-going learners once he received funding for his proposal.

At the time of writing, Herman was father to a five-year-old boy. He was in a relationship with the mother of the child, although they did not live together. In talking about being a father, he said he had a close bond with his child, whom he saw every day. He felt happy about the closeness of his relationship with his partner, who was completing a Master's degree at a university in Johannesburg at the time. He echoed Martin's opinion that it was possible 'for one to grow up in Alexandra and still be different boy', although he acknowledged that the process of being a different boy was not easy. He reflected on his experiences as a young school-going boy who was teased by *tsotsi* boys, even as he managed to navigate the terrain and maintain a balance between being studious but also 'cool', which he described as unpleasant at times. Having a strong and solid sense of his own identity had helped him, he said, and allowed him to resist peer pressure that might have led to damaging risk-taking behaviour. He hoped to be a positive father figure to his boy child not to fall for any peer pressure and said he would be open in talking to him about questions of masculinity, especially positive voices. Not growing up with his father had certainly affected him, he acknowledged, but he also felt that, despite this, he had managed to become a better man.

Themba's story

I met Themba when he was 15 years old and set on improving his considerable skills with a soccer ball. I had ten individual follow-up interviews with him. Although he was not as strong academically as some of the other boys, he worked hard and got his matric. Financial problems precluded him from pursuing tertiary education and so after leaving school he began looking for a job. He did not find this easy at all and he was unemployed for almost two years before securing a position as a salesperson. One of the things he had to deal with in the job market was the negative stereotype that labelled young black men from Alexandra as potential criminals.

'I was working for this company,' he told me in an interview one winter weekend over a steaming cup of tea. 'There were only four of us from Alexandra but the rest of people were from other regions. It was funny because this company is next to Alex. It is not making sense. Why do we have so many people from other regions? He said Alex people are not good. I started off as a clerk in the back room where everything happens. They had to move me because I am from Alex.' He gave me a wry smile. 'Luckily, stealing is not in my head.'

Recognising his work ethic, the company sent him on some IT short courses and eventually he got promoted. However, in 2012 he was retrenched and for two years after that he could not find work. He described being unemployed as the most depressing period of his life. He was sad but remained optimistic about finding a new job. Because he had experience in the IT sector, he was hired by another company to work in their graphic design division, where he was supported and mentored. He attended various short courses to acquire more skills and knowledge. At the time of writing, he was working as a digital specialist in the company. His view was that 'dedication in life does pay off'. He explained that he had learned while growing up that dreams come and go. He had once been an aspiring soccer player with a bright future, and was selected to play at a soccer tournament in the United Kingdom. On his return, he suffered a major injury that meant he was no longer able to play. However, he did not lose hope but instead shifted his attention to his schoolwork until he completed matric. He was happy to be working and assisting his family financially. He hoped his younger brother would do well at school and go on to study at a university, as he had been unable to do.

Themba had a four-year-old daughter but was separated from the mother of his child. He tried hard to be a good father to his daughter, he told me, but the relationship with his ex-partner did not make it easy for him to see his child regularly. After he lost his job, she took the child away. 'It affected me badly,' he admitted. 'I was angry ... My child was my first love. Besides any other one, that was my true love. I learned to love her with all my heart.'

Being denied access to his daughter caused him a lot of pain and he expressed confusion and bewilderment about the situation, maintaining his commitment to doing what he could to contribute to supporting her.

'The other family does not want to. So I do not know where the problem lies because I truly wanna pay for everything. I truly wanna pay for my daughter's school fees, anything that has to do with her, I wanna pay for it. She is mine; I do not expect anyone to do that. So, I even got to a point where I can marry the child and not the mother as a tradition. They still would not allow me. We went to court and they said they are going to review it and my mom attends the matter because I told her it is going to disturb me mentally and spiritually.'

It was obvious that Themba felt frustrated by the lack of access to his daughter. He wanted to be part of her life but this was not possible. He often appeared to be depressed when we discussed this issue. He agreed that it was a part of his life that he did not want to talk about as it reminded him of his pain at being unable to see or spend time with his daughter. He challenged the dominant view that men tend to be absent in their children's lives, saying, 'This is not true. What do you call me, absent father or what? Can you call me absent father? I'm not absent but I'm absent. It is not absent by choice but by force.'

Grace Khunou unpacks the meaning of absent fatherhood and argues that it is common for fathers to be denied access to their children.[9] Her findings indicate that the judiciary does not help such fathers, compared to the help provided to mothers when maintenance cases are lodged. Khunou's view is that the judiciary needs to be transformed to deal with changing gender relations in South Africa.[10] As argued by Eddy Mazembo Mavungu, Hayley Thomson-de Boor and Karabo Mphaka, fathers cannot simply be reduced to being providers of money, as some, like Themba, wish to have a close emotional relationship with their children as well.[11]

Themba was especially frustrated that the court process was taking longer than he had expected. His consolation was in trying to be a good father to his new partner's son, who was six years old. He described their relationship as close, adding that they played together and enjoyed each other's company. He asserted that he felt 'blessed in some other things, she has a son. It is a chance to groom that child – even if it is not mine, but God graced me with something – that this is an opportunity that I have missed for so long. It doesn't have to be my own child to say he is my child.' Here, Themba does not limit the status of 'fatherhood' to the biological process, instead suggesting the social and psychological role that older brothers or other men might play in children's lives. However, in the process of loving his stepson, he had to deal with his current partner's fears and anxieties about men as serial cheaters. Her previous dating experience had led to her feeling this way and he knew he had to work hard to convince her that she could trust and rely on him.

'In her eyes there is this stigma that men are trash,' he told me. 'Thanks God I turned out the way I did. She sees a different kind of man. I initiate a lot of heart-to-heart conversations with her. I do not want to hide away from her. I tell her what is at the depth of my heart at any given time. If I feel today I am going to tell her how much I love her, I tell her and then I do little gestures, buy her flowers. Let's go out for ice-cream. Let's do all the girly things, let's not do what I wanna do, let's do all your girly things.' He gave a small chuckle at the revelation. 'We're fine. But still the perception is still like that men are trash and the trash part, aah, men are dogs. She is sceptical that one day I would see another woman or something, which is true because life is like that but not me. At the level of mine I am a good man. I just speak out. There are a few of us that are very good, that are very honest about – if we love you, we love you.'

bell hooks would no doubt be impressed by the capacity of some young black men to express their deepest feelings of love and care for their partners.[12] Themba rejected the notion that men cannot express feelings of love. He was open about how he felt and how much he loved his partner, but acknowledged that being a 'different' man was hard work as young black men faced many challenges, especially the temptation to use drugs and drink heavily. He told a story about meeting a former schoolmate. He recounted that he initially did not recognise him because he kept calling Themba '*grootman, grootman* [older brother]'.

At what must have been my puzzed expression, he explained further.

His former classmate, he said, was clearly addicted to drugs, loitering on the streets and asking for money. 'It was very disturbing to me that my own age group is calling me *grootman* because I look clean, shave and smell good and he does not have those things and he calls me *grootman*.'

For Themba, it was a reflective moment and he grew pensive. Young men needed to think about their actions, he said after a few moments, 'because we will reap what we sow later in life. You don't want to waste your life like this guy, thinking you are clever smoking and drinking. Yes, you can drink but drink responsibly ... calling your peers or boys younger than you *grootman*. It is not right.'

Themba was one of the boys who felt he had benefited on a personal development level from the research project in which he had been an active participant. It had been life-changing for him, he told me. He thought it was important for mentorship programmes to be arranged and developed for boys and men to talk about the daily challenges they encounter.

It is possible to draw some positive conclusions from the attitudes of the young fathers who shared their insights with me. Perhaps young men are beginning to embrace the image of the 'new age father', which involves moving away from solely playing the traditional breadwinner role and moving towards a role characterised by emotional care, love and concern for their children. Not all young fathers are neglecting their duty to love and care for their children, despite the many challenges that some encounter in their daily lives.

These new voices of positive fatherhood need to be promoted and celebrated publicly.

9 | 'I'm Still Hopeful, Still Positive' – Holding onto a Dream

That adolescent boys encounter difficulties and challenges as they negotiate their masculinity is not in doubt. All the boys in my study negotiated their masculinities differently in their transition from being adolescents to young men. My intention to go further, to explore how young men made this transition over a long period of time and growing up as they did in a South African township environment, characterised by poverty, overcrowding and with no guarantee of basic amenities, delivered inspiring stories as well as some distressing ones. Some of the boys in my study managed to deal with these challenges, but others lost focus along the way. Some struggled to see a way through or around the many difficulties they encountered. Some watched with anger, sadness and regret as these obstacles derailed their life plans.

Simon's story

As with the other boys, I first met and interviewed Simon when he was an adolescent. He was 15 years old and already an impressive, intelligent young man, highly articulate and confident in himself. He had a clear idea of what it meant to be a young male who was 'different'. He was one of the most reflective boys in the research project and embraced what I considered to be alternative, non-violent and non-sexist voices of masculinity. These alternatives were characterised by tensions and contradictions, but on the whole Simon managed to resolve them healthily.

When he was in high school, he identified as an academic boy who was also Christian.

Simon was one of the boys who grew up without a father in his life, but he had three older brothers he looked up to and whom he saw as father figures. In one of our interviews he said: 'When I grow I wish to be a good father, especially when I have a boy child so that I can treat him how I wanted to be treated as a little boy.'

According to Simon's mother, his father left when Simon was three weeks old. Simon spoke about his wish to meet his father but also accepted that this would probably never happen as his father had never bothered to visit him, despite knowing where he lived. He indicated that he 'just [needed] to accept the situation that my father would never come and visit me. My mother has been encouraging [me] to forget my father.' Convincing himself to give up on the hope of meeting his father was not an easy process emotionally, however. 'Like, I used to ask my mother, is he a nice guy?' he said wistfully in one of our interviews. 'And my mother used to say negative things about him. And then at times I used to say maybe she is saying this because he does not live with me and all that. But I think I am starting to believe those things, that he was not such a great guy.'

Understandably, perhaps, in part Simon might well have attributed his mother's negative comments about his father to her anger and bitterness at having been abandoned by him with a small child. He thought she might have been biased in her assessment of the man as a result. However, Simon slowly began to believe that his father might not be such a 'good person' after all and seemed more willing to relinquish his fantasy of meeting him. He appreciated his mother's explanation that his father had never shown any interest in forming a meaningful relationship with him and he should thus forget about him. In any event Simon had little choice but to develop some way of coping that involved abandoning images of his absent father and accepting that his father was not interested in him.

Simon also spoke about his mother and the role she played in supporting him. She was central to his life. 'I would not be who I am if it was not [for] my mother,' he claimed more than once. 'I can say she is my hero.' He described her as a hardworking person who had managed to support all of her children without help from anyone. Consequently, he saw her as his role model and because of the solidity of his mother as a very present figure in his world and his attesting to this, this suggests that he did not feel any sense of emptiness in respect of his absent father. At the time of completing this book, his mother remained a central figure in his life and continued to support him.

As a 15-year-old, Simon spoke about other boys boasting about their fathers at high school. 'Sometimes at school most of the time, people are, like, talking about their fathers and you can't jump into that conversation because you never lived with your father.' He felt fortunate in this situation because he had older brothers. 'But then, still, on my side I could talk about my brothers,' he said, 'because most of my friends it's, like, their mothers, their fathers and them. You see, a brother from a father is quite different, but then for my side my brothers filled spaces like a father. I never got to live with my father, and all that. So my brothers, I take them like my fathers, my second fathers. I never had that opportunity to, like, sit with my father but my brothers were able to fill up that space of my father.'

In regarding his three brothers as a positive replacement for his absent father, the status of 'fatherhood' was extended to the social and psychological role that older brothers or other men may play in young boys' lives. This emerged clearly in Simon's narrative when he emphasised that his three brothers were his 'second fathers', filling the gap that had been left by his father leaving. He saw his brothers as positive male role models. Tragically, two months after our first interview in 2007, I received a call from Simon telling me that one of his brothers had been shot dead in Alexandra. In my follow-up interview with him to discuss his brother's death, he said with considerable emotion that losing his brother was like losing his father: 'You still remember when I talked to you the last time I told you that I see my brothers as my fathers. Yeah, now I feel like I lost another father.' It was an emotionally charged conversation and I needed to assist Simon to process his grief at this sudden loss. In this interview, he emphasised that he had regarded his brother as his father because he had advised and guided him on what it meant to be a responsible boy who did not engage in risk-taking behaviours.

Simon's experience in this regard confirms Nhlanhla Mkhize's view that in traditional African families, fatherhood is the collective social responsibility of all male members of the household (brothers in Simon's case) and other members of the extended family, including grandparents and uncles.[1] All these male figures play an important role in socialising adolescent boys into what it means to be an African boy and, later, a man. In follow-up interviews in 2007 and 2008, Simon told me he was still struggling to accept his brother's death and he was highly emotional when speaking about him. He felt this loss had left a big gap in his soul. Despite these emotional struggles, Simon was positive about his masculine identity as a young boy. He had strong views about how boys needed to behave in order to avoid any involvement in risk-taking behaviours. Like some of the other boys, he also spoke about his future fantasies of being a good father. In one of our interviews, in the context of discussing his disappointment with his own experience of being fathered, I asked Simon what kind of father he would want to be.

Simon was emphatic in his answer. 'A father that is always there for his son,' he said, adding quickly,

> if I have a son. I want to be always, always, always there. I want to spend most of my time with my child. Even if I work on Saturdays and Sundays. Make time. Whatever job I do I must make time for my child. Even if I work a simple job eight to five; even if I have work to do, I must make time to ask, What did you do at school today? and all that. Because that thing affects a child. This thing affects ... you know when you say to your dad, I'm just speaking generally, when you say to your dad, Hey, Dad I heard this and this, and then your dad is focusing on his work and he is not interested in what you are saying. It affects that kid because they want to spend that time with their daddy.

'Why do you wish to have a boy?' I asked him.

This time Simon thought for a few minutes and his reply was a poignant one: 'To relive that life, refill that space, re-act that life, making my son me and I would be my father. But then acting it the way I would have loved it to be. Not the way it would have been, but acting it the way I would have loved it to be.'

Simon was emphatic in his views about the importance of fathers spending time with their children. Children need paternal interest, he insisted. They need attention, love and care. He embraced an alternative understanding of 'fatherhood' – that it was not only the mother's duty to help children manage their daily lives but that the father should also make time to bond with his children and engage with their emotional needs and concerns. As a researcher, I found Simon to be thoughtful in his reflections. His fantasies about fatherhood were based largely on being a 'different' father to his own absent father. That he hoped to have a son in particular was interesting on a psychological level. I wondered whether having a son would help Simon fill the gap caused by his own unmet emotional needs as a young boy. His conversation about fathering confirmed this with his insight that he wanted to 'act it the way I would have loved it to be'.

In their research Mary Target and Peter Fonagy found that parents often live their unfulfilled needs through their children, and this was borne out for me by Simon expressing this longing, in a projected fantasy of the future, to make up for his ungratified needs by meeting the needs of his own son.[2] A baby boy would help him 'relive that life, refill that space'. Michael Diamond sees such a wish as a compensatory mechanism to help the individual fulfil his childhood fantasy of having a loving and caring father.[3] Clearly, for Simon this was a psychic fantasy, to fulfil himself through producing, claiming and caring for a son. It indicates that the lack of a positive fathering experience may engender the desire to become a 'different' father and to undo the pain that one suffered as a child. Psychoanalytic writers such as Peter Blos argue that fatherhood represents an opportunity for men to heal from their own woundedness in relation to how they were fathered.[4] Being a father reactivates repressed traumas, which need to be worked through.

Simon did not get the opportunity to be a father. He was arrested in 2014 before he had a child and sentenced in 2017 to 13 years' imprisonment. He reflected on this in one of our meetings while in prison, saying that he was disappointed with how things had turned out. He felt that he had failed to fulfil many of his dreams.

At the time of our first interview in 2007, Simon was in Grade 11. He described himself (and was described by other boys) as an academic boy and he was known in his neighbourhood for being studious and committed to his schoolwork. He worked extremely hard to do well at school and rejected the notion of violent township masculinity associated with boys in Alexandra. He was somewhat surprised that *tsotsi* boys were more popular at school than 'good' boys like him. He said, 'You see many of these guys [*tsotsi* boys] are bullies, but failures at school. They are failures, you know, when it comes to schoolwork. They get zeros in tests and assignments.' He saw himself as different compared to *tsotsi* boys and he also disagreed with the dominant view that boys should have multiple partners, lamenting the fact that having multiple partners tarnished the image of 'good' boys because then girls saw all boys as the same in only wanting to have sex with girls and nothing else.

'Yeah, I feel like you must have one,' he affirmed, 'because you must be honest and loyal to your girlfriend. Because when you are with her, you will be telling her, you are only the heart of my desire. But you know very well that she is not the only one. So I think we must be faithful to our lovers.'

His view was that boys should show commitment to one girlfriend and not prioritise sex in such relationships. He disclosed that he was a virgin due to his religious beliefs as a Christian ('the Bible says sex before marriage is sin'), acknowledging that this sometimes meant he was a target for scorn, although he seemed able to stand his ground. 'Boys they take you like a fool when you go to church,' he said at that first interview with a small smile. There were many other neighbourhood pressures from his peers, such as smoking or drinking. Simon confessed that he used to do both but stopped after becoming a born-again Christian. Referring to his friends when he was smoking and drinking, he explained: 'I was pleasing them or pleasing anyone.' Interestingly, while he had stopped engaging in these behaviours, many of his friends did not know he had stopped for the simple reason that he hadn't told them. This demonstrated that he was concerned about losing his status as a 'cool' guy if his friends found out, but he also displayed a certain independence when he said, 'I actually do not care anymore ... yeah, the coolness and the status doesn't worry me anymore because at first it used to worry me.'

This reflects something of the internal battle Simon was experiencing. On the one hand it seems that he was worried about being ostracised and on the other, perhaps, also of appearing to be judgemental. He still wanted to maintain the image of being a 'cool' boy, despite occupying different and even contradictory positions. However, he also acknowledged that occasionally he felt confused about his identity and often found the process of being in the 'borderland' overwhelming, taxing and energy consuming. He confessed in an individual interview with me that sometimes he had feelings of self-doubt in his interactions with his male peers. However, initially he continued to spend time with them and was able to resist their peer pressure, although this involved some self-sacrifice and self-discipline. He described one occasion when he felt conflicted and also how he handled it.

'They offered me a drink, and I was, like, confident – I'm, like, no, no I'm fine. And then I kept quiet. After a while, I thought about taking the drink and then I said to my friends, Guys, I would be back now. Then I went home. And then I sat down, never went out again.'

Simon did not want to disappoint his friends by refusing to drink, but it was equally clear that he wanted to drink too – hence the internal conflicting conversation in his mind. Going home was an escape for him and helped him resist the impulse to drink. He had to remove himself from the situation in order to manage these tensions rather than engage his peers directly. The internal battle of resisting the temptation to drink and smoke was intertwined with a deeper fear of failing himself should he give in to the temptation, something else he acknowledged dryly, with honesty and insight.

'Yeah, you know sometimes you can't help temptation. Temptation just comes everywhere. So instead of being in that situation where you are going to be tempted, just be out of it completely ... yeah, it's a battle at first. But when you get used to the idea, it becomes something that you live with. You wouldn't even be tempted at all to drink at all! But when it's, like, a few months that you have stopped this thing; it's a battle. It's, like, a tough battle.'

Simon was always insightful and reflective in his interviews, confirming Gary Barker's view that the achievement of alternative masculine identities requires boys to have well-developed self-reflective abilities.[5] Simon had some of these abilities, as the way he resolved the situation around the temptation to drink with his friends demonstrates and also the way he explained his thinking in our interview. This suggested that he had found strategies to manage this, but he did not minimise his vulnerabilities and struggles. His narratives were authentic and he had a clear sense of self, although many times confesssed that being a 'different' boy was a 'tough battle'.

Simon spoke about the coping strategies he used to deal with some of his internal conflicts. He asserted that being a Christian helped him handle a range of 'temptations', including the temptation to have sex. Many of his photos were creative and imaginative and featured activities at church. In commenting on them, Simon mentioned that an internal voice guided him in resisting the temptations that life threw at him. He said repeatedly that it was against the teachings of Christianity to smoke, drink alcohol and have sex before marriage. Religion thus played a key role in helping Simon cope with some of his internal conflicts. He had internalised these Christian values and used them to guide his behaviour. At the same time, his desires and impulses seemed to be repressed in that he associated premarital sex with sin. Religion forced him to repress his sexual desires, but this was accompanied by some fear of disintegrating and losing his sense of self. Simon 'confessed' to being an ambivalent masculine subject. He was the boy who had been tempted to have sex with his girlfriend and was on the verge of submitting to it when his sister arrived home. When the sex did not happen, it left him feeling relieved that he had managed to control his sexual urges.

Religious beliefs, teachings and mores may thus help adolescent boys to exercise self-control in abstaining from sexual activity, despite the fact that managing this kind of prohibition may in itself be anxiety provoking.[6] As can be seen in some of his reflections, Simon was different to many other boys in Alexandra.

Simon passed matric with good marks but was not able to go on to a tertiary institution due to lack of finances at home. He spent the whole of 2010 at home, which he experienced as a frustrating and stressful period. 'At this stage,' told me in an interview, the distress showing on his face, 'my frustrations were high because everything I seemed to try out failed. I really wanted to go to the university, but nothing worked in raising money. I lost focus along the way.'

Simon was extremely emotional when he spoke about this part of his life. As he saw it, he became weak and, succumbing to the pressure of money, he started hanging out with a 'wrong crowd' – referring to his peers who were involved in criminal activities. He also got involved in these activities, he said – 'I found myself living off criminal activities' – but added, significantly: 'If my brother was still alive, I wouldn't be here.' He was quick to correct himself, taking responsibility for his behaviour, not blaming 'everything' on the death of his brother, although the pain of that loss still rested heavily on him. 'His guidance and role was very vital in my life,' he said.

I did follow-up interviews with him in prison after his arrest, before his case came to court and also afterwards. He shared with me that he was terrified on his first day in prison and did not know what to expect as he had heard so many stories of violence among inmates before he was arrested. Fights among inmates were common, he said, but fortunately he himself had never been a victim. It took him weeks to adjust to what he described as poor living conditions of sleeping on a bunk bed, and sharing a cell with 50 to 60 other inmates in a space designed for 10 to 20 inmates. His adjustment to the prison environment was not easy but he said he was managing.

In one of our follow-up interviews, I gave him copies of the transcripts of the interviews I conducted with him before he was arrested. He confided that he got very depressed when he read them, especially the positive view he had had about himself and life in general. 'I was disgusted when I read transcripts of some of our interviews when I was still young,' he said. 'It seems I had dreams – and big dreams. All is gone. I ask myself what happened.'

He told me that he had been using his time in prison to reflect and think about himself. He said: 'I discovered a lot of things about myself while here. There are days when I sit in my cell and never go any[where]. Though I lost focus I did not die inside. I'm [a] very strong person. Being here in prison has made [me] very strong ... When I think who I was that I'm now, it breaks my heart. You feel like rewinding the clock but there is nothing one can do. You just need to sit and think about the future.'

He spoke at length about what he felt about his imprisonment and how this affected him daily. He was worried that he had disappointed his mother. 'When I see my mother cry when she visits me in prison [it] breaks my heart. I hold my mother in my mind all the time. She lives in my mind. She continues to be the figure that holds me. I get strength from her.' Despite his imprisonment, his mother continued to be a central figure in his life. She made time to visit and brought him all the items he needed. He regarded his mother as the only person who still believed in him.

On one occasion when I visited him in prison, Simon gave me a letter. Entitled 'Conversation with Self', I reproduce it here, unedited:

I wake up every morning asking myself how I got here. I wake up every morning asking myself how I lost that burning desire that once resided in me. I often don't have answers but today it struck me, it struck me real hard. You lost focus, Simon, No I did not! Yes you did. These two things pop up and get a sense of being in denial. Well who wouldn't be in denial of personal blame of waking in this place (prison) every day. I dream of this place. I wake up in this place. Have I become part of this place? Have altered my DNA and created a whole different person? Is this my new reality? No. You wake up one day not feeling well whether it's physical, emotional or mental. You just not up for the day. In these instances one simply puts on the pretend face and just gets through the day. I hate pretending but in order to respect other people I have to act strong and okay while all the time I'm putting on an act. I'm learning so much in these processes from personal things to things about human character. Think of it in this way I have lived with a total of 50 or + men on a daily basis in one cell with one urinal, one toilet, and one shower. What more can a man teach me? The other day I was reflecting back in my life tracking my trails on who I have been and who I am and where I have been and where I am. From the boy that I once dreamt of being an Engineer (civil), a boy that loved and respected his moral values to sitting in a prison cell. Yes I said it, a prison cell. Whenever I walk to the toilet I ask myself that I needed my faults to find myself but it saddens me because this price of finding myself is tough. The toughness I'm referring to has many elements. Having to pay officials a certain fee is tough, having to adjust to the food is tough, having to deal with others is tough, and having to witness sodomy is tough. One of the toughest elements is having your spirit and belief system tarnished and questioned. Living amongst people who have a different belief system than yours is very tough.

A lot has been written about South African prisons, especially the issue of overcrowding and the problems associated with this, including gang violence.[7] I noted earlier that before Simon was arrested, I had found him to be an insightful boy with the ability to think and reflect about himself. Reading his letter reminded me of our conversations while he was still in high school. Even then, he had the ability to reflect and be introspective about what it meant to be a boy and he had questioned many hegemonic masculine practices.

His letter gave us the opportunity to delve into a number of issues, including his coping mechanisms (writing, prayer and self-talk) to deal with the challenges in the prison environment, which he described as characterised by violent acts among fellow inmates due to toxic masculinities. He said it was hard to live under those conditions, but he was trying to remain positive and clear his mind. He acknowledged that there were moments when he felt weak and demotivated but he also acknowledged that prison had 'revived the old me'. He continues to write letters (which are too many to publish in this book) about his feelings and emotions, all entitled Conversations with Self. He says these 'conversations' help him 'make peace with the past but they also bring about a sombre mood at times ... [I] also do self-introspection to learn from my mistakes'. For example, he told me, he had made a conscious decision not to join any prison gang as he felt this would betray what he had stood for before he was arrested. His arrest, he said, had given him much time to think and reflect about his life and future plans.

At the time of writing this book, Simon was registered for an LLB degree and had been moved to another prison where he described conditions as 'better' and allowed him to study. 'Studying towards my LLB degree is the first step in turning my life around,' he said. 'I'm still hopeful, still positive. My focus is on rising from strength to strength, as hard as it is.' He did not blame his friends for the predicament in which he now found himself. He accepted that he had had the agency to say no to certain things but had been unable to do so. At that time, as he described it, his self 'had disappeared ... and got lost in the world of instant gratification'. He knew he would continue to experience the same internal battles in prison, but was determined to focus on his future goals by studying and completing his degree. He saw his imprisonment as a second life opportunity to grow and be a different person – the man he was before he got arrested.

10 | Safe Spaces –
Listening, Hearing, Action

Inevitably there came a day when the 'official' part of my longitudinal research project came to an end and there was much professional satisfaction for me in that. On a personal level, however, I had long since realised that my encounters with these young men had affected and changed me. I had not just tracked these boys as participants in an academic research work. I had accompanied them on their journey as they transitioned from school-going boys to young men entering the world of work, forming solid intimate relationships (no more *cherries*, only *regtes*), getting married, having children and being fathers themselves. They had allowed me access to how their identities as young black men shifted and changed at key points in their lives. I got to know and care about many of them on a deep personal level.

My interactions with these boys and young men mobilised feelings in them as well, just as they did in me. At times I found myself over-identifying with participants' feelings of anger and disappointment with their absent fathers, especially when a father was unknown as in my own case. I had to work through these feelings during this research project. I think being a psychologist helped me to manage my reactions, which I have never shared with the boys, nor with colleagues that worked with over the years. I used my journal to record the feelings, which I hope to share on another platform in the future.

In the individual and follow-up interviews, the boys stated that they felt the research questions touched on issues that were very private and personal, such as relationships with their absent fathers and the deaths of loved ones. As a result, there were instances when some boys cried during the interviews. This was a very difficult part of the research process. My professional training as a counselling psychologist helped me to contain their feelings and emotions, although it was not always easy to respond to their emotions as a psychologist while still fulfilling my role as a researcher. This was an unavoidable tension that I often had to manage as some of the participants had pressing personal difficulties that they wanted to share with me as part of their personal struggle to negotiate their identities. I thus became very involved in some of these boys' personal lives.

For example, when Marcus disclosed to me that he was gay, I felt helpless when he described the difficulties he faced as a result and the discrimination and abuse he had to endure daily. Our interview sessions were therefore also used as a debriefing opportunity to talk about his fears and anxieties. He reflected later in a follow-up meeting as a young adult that those earlier meetings had provided him some relief and support. He had felt alone and 'hated being gay due to discrimination' until he started talking to me about his feelings.

Another boy phoned to tell me he had failed. He cried over the phone and I had to calm him down. I arranged a face-to-face meeting to debrief and encourage him not to lose hope and to repeat the grade, which he did, successfully passing the year.

I can provide countless examples of instances when I had to be more intimately involved in these boys' lives than I had initially anticipated. However, all these interactions provided useful data on the emotional worlds of these young men, which also facilitated a deeper understanding on my part about the difficulties they encountered in their everyday lives.

I had mixed feelings and emotions about this final stage of the research process. I was excited and happy to see that some of the boys had become 'responsible' young men, achieving the dreams that they had shared with me while they were still in high school. However, I was also sad to see that others had failed to achieve their full potential due to all kinds of adverse circumstances.

In what I hope will become a useful contribution to the field of masculinities research, alongside that of many colleagues – South African and international – I need first to summarise what my longitudinal research project in Alexandra township and its subsequent reshaping into this book has shown me – and therefore the reader. More importantly, however, my interest and further plan is to consider and then suggest what practical strategies and interventions might be put in place in a township environment in order for this research to be more meaningful. I want to use these findings to inform public policies and intervention strategies aimed at helping boys and men in South Africa to develop masculine identities that are healthy and non-violent. I have already started this work by organising community meetings with boys and young men to discuss various issues relating to masculinities and the positive role that men can play to prevent various forms of violence in their respective communities.

*

Being an adolescent boy and adopting the masculine identity of a 'real' boy is a complicated process, one that is often characterised by contradictions and feelings of ambivalence. Some versions of masculinity (for example, *tsotsi* boys or *sex-jaro* boys) are more valued and celebrated than others (academic or Christian-oriented, for example) that are non-risk taking, non-violent and, to some extent, non-sexist. The process of negotiating these multiple and conflicting voices of masculinity is not easy.

Through the many interview sessions I conducted over the period with the boys selected for the project, and as they matured into young men, it became evident to me that there were different ways of being a boy and certain identities were more dominant or central for some boys than for others. The boys did not fit neatly into the typologies identified in the study. For some boys, identification with a certain type of masculinity remained quite consistent but many vacillated between multiple positions, simultaneously accepting and rejecting certain aspects of township masculinity. Many of them straddled a range of masculine positions in order to maintain a particular reputation and status in their peer group. They managed this fairly effectively but also experienced it as emotionally exhausting and often frustrating.

The participants were aware of a hierarchy of masculinities in which alignment with some positions rather than others allows for social status and positive self-esteem. In this respect, certain 'types' of masculinity occupy either hegemonic or counter-hegemonic status among township boys. Two identities that enjoy largely hegemonic status are *tsotsi* masculinity, associated with defiance, toughness, risk taking and willingness to engage in interpersonal violence, and *sex-jaro* masculinity, associated with a virile sexuality and having multiple girlfriends as sex partners.

However, a significant proportion of the boys in my study resisted the celebration of these identities and demonstrated a willingness to take up alternative positions. This resistance was often not overt, but in many instances took the form of future-oriented fantasies to achieve certain career and other goals. In these imagined futures, some boys fantasised about an inversion of existing power relations, where they would become superior to boys whose current social positioning was more popular than theirs. On the whole, the findings revealed the considerable internal and external struggles that boys experience in adopting both popular and unpopular masculine positions.

A further finding was that all the boys, irrespective of 'type', were united in their antagonism towards 'gay masculinity', accusing gay boys of letting males down in a variety of ways. It was evident in all the interviews that gay masculinity occupies a very low status in the hierarchy of masculinities. This was despite some interviewees purporting to be more accepting of homosexuality than others, although they still expressed rather conservative and prejudicial attitudes in this respect. The boys used various techniques, including drawing on popularised religious, cultural and medical discourses, to support their views that being gay was not normal – a view challenged by the two gay men in the study, who managed to assert their gay identities by openly living their lives, despite continuous challenges of homophobia and stigma.

It was evident that having relationships with girls is important, although the importance of these relationships differs from one group of boys to another. For *sex-jaro* boys, having sex with girls is a key priority, although actual sexual encounters may be threatening to their sense of manhood as many may privately be worried about their ability to satisfy girls sexually. For males clearly sex is a source of power but simultaneously it produces feelings of fear and anxiety. Other boys reject the view that sex should be a priority in relationships with girls and many of the boys who hold this view value their virginity, although feelings of ambivalence and self-doubt are often prevalent. These boys risk being teased or treated with derision by other boys.

The majority of boys in the study grew up without father figures. Despite this, many expressed the desire and some commitment to being 'different' and 'good' fathers. Generally, the participants spoke about their mothers as positive role models, which is contrary to much of the existing literature in which female-headed households are often presented as a source of emotional problems for many adolescent boys. In this study, mothers were frequently seen as pillars of strength and a source of comfort and emotional support.

Some of the boys in the study were able to resist, subvert and challenge the dominant norms of township masculinity in order to assert an 'alternative', non-violent, non-risk-taking and non-sexist masculinity. These were the boys who displayed high levels of self-reflection, introspection and insight about what it meant to be a 'different' young man and the determination required to maintain this stance. Being reflective and insightful, having educational aspirations and valuing academic achievement were factors that helped these boys and young men resist and reject involvement in hypermasculine behaviours that might have placed them and others at risk in various ways. It was also evident that external support, for example, from family members (especially mothers), was significant in helping them to maintain responsible male identities and to resist peer pressure to conform to popularised images of township masculinity.

On the whole, the study's findings challenge popular conceptions of young black men in townships as all potentially violent or at risk of engaging in criminal activities. The study revealed that some young men are embracing alternative masculinities, although at considerable emotional cost. It would appear that a combination of internal (for example, the ability to delay immediate gratification in order to achieve long-term goals; a clear sense of self) and external (access to supportive mentors, mothers or involved caretakers) features are important in allowing boys to take up non-conforming and non-hegemonic identities in the context of a township in South Africa today.

*

At the end of the research project, all of the participants were interested in continuing our follow-up meetings, as they experienced these as cathartic and containing. They said the interviews also helped them to reflect on their male identities and on what they wished for in life, suggesting once again that boys and young men have the capacity to think about and reflect on their identities if given a safe space in which to do so.

My concluding view is that safe spaces need to be created for boys and young men to reflect on tensions, contradictions and ambivalences associated with voices of masculinity.

Schools should be doing much more to provide a conducive environment than they are doing currently and here, too, teachers have immensely important roles to play. Generally, males are given little opportunity to think about their masculinity. Intervention programmes therefore need to be developed and implemented at schools (and beyond) to assist and support boys and young men to negotiate the multiple voices of masculinity. These should be safe spaces where they can freely express their views on their gender identity without fear of criticism and ridicule. They should be supported to question, challenge and subvert notions of hegemonic masculinity that are overly constraining or are associated with risk-taking and harmful behaviours. In this way, alternative masculinities that are non-violent and non-risk-taking may emerge.

Currently, the life skills programmes offered in schools appear to be too generic. There is a need for sex health education in and out of schools, targeting adolescent boys. However, it is important that such programmes challenge common heterosexist practices in which males treat women as sex objects. The boys and young men in this study indulged in risky sexual behaviours in order to gain approval from their male peers. It is therefore important that these practices are continuously interrogated. Many of the interviews produced material indicating that adolescent boys might benefit from sex education, including education that questions traditional notions of masculinity – in particular that sexual performance is critical to affirm and validate this identity.

Furthermore, teachers and parents need to be honest and comfortable in talking to adolescent boys about sex and sexuality. They should create 'safe spaces' at home and at school where boys can discuss sex. Top-down approaches or scare tactics do not work when attempting to control boys' and young men's sexual practices. It is important for dialogical and open conversations to be held with boys and young men so that they are given the opportunity freely to express their views without fear of judgement.

Teachers need to be proactive in dealing with issues of homophobia at schools. Their silence on the topic reinforces the negative portrayal of same-sex relations as deviant, pathological and un-African. Such constructions must be challenged and interrogated within the school environment with the aim of creating the space for 'gay' boys to come to terms with their identities and lifestyle choices. These conversations also need to go beyond school corridors and into communities, which are often characterised by highly homophobic attitudes, despite our progressive Constitution and legislation that recognises same-sex relationships.

In conjunction with making changes in schools to encourage boys to believe they have access to a safe space where they can talk, be listened to and, most importantly, be heard and validated, wherever possible the involvement of parents needs to be facilitated. Parent workshops targeted at both fathers and mothers should be set up. Fathers and other male figures should be encouraged to become actively and positively involved in their adolescent boys' lives as they have a potentially important role to play as male role models. However, the important role of mothers, who in this study were often available and accessible to their adolescent sons and enjoyed considerable respect, should not be underestimated in programmes offering community support to parents. Mothers have the ability to play a positive role in raising boy children. Often – where fathers are absent or unavailable (for a variety of reasons) as was the case in my study – they have to play dual roles, and this comes with all kinds of challenges. It is therefore important that safe spaces are created for mothers to meet and talk about their fears, anxieties, frustrations and achievements when it comes to raising boy children in the absence of father figures. Sharing these experiences may help to further demystify the view that boys always need fathers to develop healthy masculine identities. It was evident in this study that some boys, despite growing up without father figures, were able to develop positive masculine identities. Many attributed their positive masculinities to their mothers who were experienced as caring, loving, nurturing and compassionate about their daily struggles of what it meant to be a boy. So much can be learned out of public conversations with mothers on how to raise young adolescent boys who are happy and confident about their sense of self. These conversations with mothers may bring a new dimension to the conversation about masculinities, which often tend to focus only on fathers and neglected mothers. Similar to men's forums, we also need women's forums to share experiences, reflections and strategies about engaging men and boys as part of transforming toxic masculinities to alternative masculinities.

Life skills workshops and counselling services should offer spaces for adolescent boys to talk about personal problems and to reflect on their masculinity in order to gain insight into how bravado or involvement in risky behaviours may be compensatory mechanisms to hide their 'real' selves. These workshops and services should focus on boys' relationships with their parents, girls, teachers, sex, drugs, violence, stress, depression and so forth. The ultimate goal of these interventions would be to create a model of young masculinity that is non-risk-taking, non-violent and non-sexist.

Two things that my research highlighted were that alternative voices of masculinity are not publicly celebrated, and that too much attention is given to hegemonic forms of masculinity. I strongly believe it is important for positive images of alternative masculinities to be popularised in the literature and mainstream media so that new voices of masculinity can emerge and be celebrated publicly. Young boys and men need these positive male role models. It is my hope that through dialogue and affirming conversations and discussion, in formal and informal groupings, we might better support boys in becoming good men.

Notes

Chapter 1

1   Malose Langa, 'Working with Juvenile Offenders: An Evaluation of Trauma Group Intervention,' *African Safety Promotion: A Journal of Injury and Violence Prevention* 5 (2007): 63–83.
2   Gary Barker, *Dying to Be Men: Youth, Masculinity and Social Exclusion* (London: Routledge, 2005).
3   Barker, *Dying to Be Men*; Steffen Jensen, *Gangs, Politics and Dignity in Cape Town* (Johannesburg: Wits University Press, 2008); Kopano Ratele, *Liberating Masculinities* (Cape Town: HSRC Press, 2016).
4   A popular shop where liquor and meat are sold.

Chapter 2

1   Stephen Frosh, Ann Phoenix and Rob Pattman, *Young Masculinities: Understanding Boys in Contemporary Society* (New York: Palgrave, 2002); Tamara Shefer, Kopano Ratele, Anna Strebel, Nonhlanhla Shabalala and Rosemarie Buikema, *From Boys to Men: Social Constructions of Masculinity in Contemporary Society* (Cape Town: UCT Press, 2007); Deevia Bhana, 'Violence and the Gendered Negotiation of Masculinity among Young Black School Boys in South Africa,' in *African Masculinities: Men in Africa from the Late 19th Century to the Present*, ed. Lahoucine Ouzgane and Robert Morrell (Pietermaritzburg: University of KwaZulu-Natal Press; New York: Palgrave Macmillan, 2005); Eric Anderson, *Inclusive Masculinity: The Changing Nature of Masculinities* (New York: Routledge, 2010).
2   Raewyn W Connell, *Masculinities* (Cambridge: Polity Press, 1995), 65.
3   Robert Morrell, *Changing Men in Southern Africa* (Pietermaritzburg: University of Natal Press, 2001), 33.
4   Antonio Gramsci, *Selections from the Prison Notebooks* (New York: International Publishers, 1971).

5   Connell, *Masculinities*, 77.

6   Connell, *Masculinities*.

7   Arthur Brittan, *Masculinity and Power* (Oxford: Basil Blackwell, 1989); Michael Moller, 'Exploiting Patterns: A Critique of Hegemonic Masculinity,' *Journal of Gender Studies* 16 (2007); Mike Donaldson, 'What Is Hegemonic Masculinity?,' *Theory and Society* 22 (1993); Demetrakis Demetriou, 'Connell's Concept of Hegemonic Masculinity: A Critique,' *Theory and Society* 30 (2001).

8   Demetriou, 'Connell's Concept,' 341.

9   Margaret Wetherell and Nigel Edley, 'Negotiating Hegemonic Masculinity,' *Feminism and Psychology* 9 (1999).

10 Raewyn W Connell, 'Hegemonic Masculinity: Rethinking the Concept,' *Gender and Society* 19 (2005).

11 Connell, *Masculinities*; Wetherell and Edley, 'Negotiating Hegemonic Masculinity'.

12 Demetriou, 'Connell's Concept,' 355.

13 Robert Morrell, Rachel Jewkes and Graham Lindegger, 'Hegemonic Masculinity/Masculinities in South Africa', *Culture, Power and Gender Politics* 15 (2012).

14 Kopano Ratele, 'Subordinate Black South African Men without Fear,' *Cahiers d'études Africaines* 53 (2013).

15 Bhana, 'Violence and Gendered Negotiation'; Deevia Bhana, 'What Matters to Girls and Boys in a Black Primary School in South Africa,' *Early Child Development and Care* 175 (2005).

16 Bhana, 'What Matters to Girls'.

17 Elaine Unterhalter, 'Global Inequality, Capabilities, Social Justice: The Millennium Development Goal for Gender Equality in Education,' *International Journal of Educational Development* 25 (2005).

18 Jean Redpath, Robert Morrell, Rachel Jewkes and Dean Peacock, *Masculinities and Public Policy in South Africa: Changing Masculinities and Working toward Gender Equality'* (Johannesburg: Sonke Gender Justice Network, 2008).

19 Anne Watson, Michael Kehler and Wayne Martino, 'The Problem of Boys' Literacy Underachievement: Raising Some Questions,' *Journal of Adolescent and Adult Literacy* 53 (2010); Emma Renold, '"Other" Boys: Negotiating Non-Hegemonic Masculinities in the Primary School,' *Gender and Education* 16 (2004); Bhana, 'What Matters to Girls'; Redpath et al., *Masculinities and Public Policy*.

20 Connell, *Masculinities*; Bhana, 'Violence and the Gendered Negotiation'; Bhana, 'What Matters to Girls'.

21 Frosh, Phoenix and Pattman, *Young Masculinities*.

22 Raewyn W Connell, *The Men and the Boys* (Cambridge: Polity Press, 2000); Rob Gilbert and Pam Gilbert, *Masculinity Goes to School* (Sydney: Allen & Unwin, 1998); Bhana, 'Violence and the Gendered Negotiation'.

23 Ratele, 'Subordinate'; David Bruce, 'Danger, Threats or Just Fear,' *SA Crime Quarterly* 13 (2005); Jensen, *Gangs, Politics*.

24 Don Pinnock, *Gang Town* (Cape Town: Tafelberg, 2016).

25 Jensen, *Gangs, Politics*. Pinnock, *Gang Town*; Elaine Salo, 'Social Constructions of Masculinity on the Racial and Gendered Margins of Cape Town' in *From Boys to Men: Social Constructions of Masculinity in Contemporary Society*, ed. Tamara Shefer et al. (Cape Town: UCT Press, 2007).

26 Pinnock, *Gang Town*; Salo, 'Social Constructions'.

27 Jensen, *Gangs, Politics*. Irvin Kinness, *From Urban Street Gangs to Criminal Empires: The Changing Face of Gangs in the Western Cape* (Pretoria: Institute for Security Studies, 2000).

28 Meredith Evans, Kathryn Risher, Nompumelelo Zungu, Olive Shisana, Sizulu Moyo, David D Celentano, Brendan Maughan-Brown and Thomas M Rehle, 'Age-Disparate Sex and HIV Risk for Young Women from 2002 to 2012 in South Africa,' *Journal of the International AIDS Society* 19 (2016). Accessed 19 July 2018. Doi: 10.7448/IAS.19.1.21310; Katherine Wood and Rachel Jewkes, '"Dangerous" Love: Reflections on Violence amongst Xhosa Township Youth,' in *Changing Men in Southern Africa*, ed. Robert Morrell (Pietermaritzburg: University of Natal Press, 2005).

29 Wood and Jewkes, 'Dangerous Love,'; Deevia Bhana and Rob Pattman, 'Girls Want Money, Boys Want Virgins: The Materiality of Love amongst South African Township Youth in the Context of HIV and AIDS,' *Culture, Health & Sexuality* 13 (2011).

30 Mark Hunter, 'Masculinities, Multiple-Sexual-Partners and AIDS: The Making and Unmaking of Isoka in KwaZulu-Natal,' *Transformation: Critical Perspectives on Southern Africa* 54 (2004).

31 Bhana and Pattman, 'Girls Want Money.'

32 Terry-Ann Selikow, Bheki Zulu and Eugene Cedras, 'The Ingagara, the Regte and the Cherry: HIV/AIDS and Youth Culture in Contemporary Urban Townships,' *Agenda* 17 (2002); Bhana and Pattman, 'Girls Want Money.'

33 Selikow, Zulu and Cedras, 'The Ingagara, the Regte and the Cherry.'

34 Rachel K Jewkes, Kristin Dunkle, Mzikazi Nduna and Nwabisa Shai, 'Intimate Partner Violence, Relationship Power Inequity, and Incidence of HIV Infection in Young Women in South Africa: A Cohort Study,' *The Lancet* 376 (2010); Romi Sigsworth, *Anyone Can Be a Rapist: An Overview of Sexual Violence in South Africa* (Johannesburg: Centre for the Study of Violence and Reconciliation, 2009).

35 Gender Links, *Research: Gender Violence 'a Reality in South Africa'* (Johannesburg: Gender Links, 2012); Institute for Security Studies, 'So Why Do the Numbers Keep Rising? A Reflection on Efforts to Prevent and Respond to Domestic Violence and Rape' (paper presented at the Institute for Security Studies Seminar, Pretoria, 27 October 2011).

36 Pumla Dineo Gqola, *Rape: A South African Nightmare* (Johannesburg: Jacana Media, 2016).

37 Shefer et al., *From Boys to Men*.

38 SACENDU (South African Community Epidemiological Network of Drug Use) (2017).

39 Michael Kimmel, *Guyland: The Perilous World Where Boys Become Men* (New York: HarperCollins, 2008).

40 Connell, *The Men and the Boys*; Kopano Ratele, 'Masculinity and Male Mortality in South Africa,' *African Safety Promotion* 6 (2008).

41 World Health Organization. *Global Status Report on Road Safety 2015*. World Health Organization, 2015.

42 MRC (Medical Research Council). 'What Are the Top Causes of Death in South Africa?' Medical Research Council, 2015, accessed January 2018, http://Www.Mrc.Ac.Za/Bod/Faqdeath.Htm.

43 Àngels Carabí and Josep Armengol, *Alternative Masculinities for a Changing World* (New York: Palgrave Macmillan, 2014).

44 Reshma Sathiparsad, 'Developing Alternative Masculinities as a Strategy to Address Gender-Based Violence,' *International Social Work* 51 (2008).

45 Bob Pease, 'Reconstructing Masculinity or Ending Manhood? The Potential and Limitations of Transforming Masculine Subjectivities for Gender Equality,' in *Alternative Masculinities for a Changing World*, ed. Àngels Carabí and Josep Armengol (New York: Palgrave MacMillan, 2014).

46 Frosh, Phoenix and Pattman, *Young Masculinities*.

47 Lynne Segal, *Slow Motion: Changing Masculinities, Changing Men* (London: Virago, 1990).

48 Pamela Attwell, 'Real Boys: Concepts of Masculinity among School Teachers' (MA dissertation, University of KwaZulu-Natal, 2002).

49 Morrell, *Changing Men*.

50 Mamphela Ramphele, *Steering by the Stars: Being Young in South Africa* (Cape Town: Tafelberg, 2002).

51 Gary Barker and Christine Ricardo, *Young Men and the Construction of Masculinity in Sub-Saharan Africa: Implications for HIV/AIDS, Conflict, and Violence* (Washington, DC: World Bank, 2005); Raewyn W Connell, *The Role of Men and Boys in Achieving Gender Equality* (Brazil: United Nations, Division for the Advancement of Women, 2003); Rachel Jewkes, Michael Flood and

James Lang, 'From Work with Men and Boys to Changes of Social Norms and Reduction of Inequities in Gender Relations: A Conceptual Shift in Prevention of Violence against Women and Girls,' *The Lancet* 385 (2015); Michael Kimmel, 'Why Men Should Support Gender Equity,' *Women's Studies* 103 (2005).

52 Linda Richter and Robert Morrell, *Baba: Men and Fatherhood in South Africa* (Cape Town: HSRC Press, 2006); Morrell, *Changing Men.*

53 Richter and Morrell, *Baba,* 64.

54 Catriona Macleod, 'The Risk of Phallocentrism in Masculinities Studies: How a Revision of the Concept of Patriarchy May Help,' *Psychology in Society* 35, (2007).

55 Robert Morrell, 'Men, Masculinities and Gender Politics in South Africa: A Reply to Macleod,' *Psychology in Society* 35 (2007).

56 Ratele, 'Masculinity and Male Mortality': 26.

57 Bob Pease, 'Men as Allies in Preventing Violence against Women: Principles and Practices for Promoting Accountability,' Center for the Study of Men and Masculinities (2017).

58 Julian Henriques, Wendy Hollway, Cathy Urwin, Couze Venn and Valerie Walkerdine, *Changing the Subject: Psychology, Social Regulation, and Subjectivity* (New York: Psychology Press, 1998).

59 Wendy Hollway, *Subjectivity and Method in Psychology: Gender, Meaning and Science* (London: Sage Publications, 1989).

60 Hollway, *Subjectivity,* 25.

61 Hollway, *Subjectivity,* 29.

62 Judith Butler, *Gender Trouble: Feminism and the Subversion of Identity* (New York: Routledge, 1990).

63 Butler, *Gender Trouble,* 138.

64 Anthony Elliot, *Concepts of Self* (Cambridge: Polity Press, 2001), 31–32.

65 Stephen Frosh, *The Politics of Psychoanalysis: An Introduction to Freud and Post-Freudian Theory* (New York: New York Press, 1999).

66 Stephen Frosh, Ann Phoenix and Rob Pattman, 'Taking a Stand: Using Psychoanalysis to Explore the Positioning of Subjects in Discourse,' *British Journal of Social Psychology* 42 (2003): 39.

67 Stephen Frosh and Lisa Baraitser, 'Psychoanalysis and Psychosocial Studies,' *Psychoanalysis, Culture & Society* 13 (2008).

68 Antony Whitehead, 'Man to Man Violence: How Masculinity May Work as a Dynamic Risk Factor,' *The Howard Journal of Criminal Justice* 44 (2005.)

69 Ratele, 'Subordinate'.

70 Jacques Lacan, *Les Complexes Familiaux (Family Complexes)* (Paris: Seuil, 1984).

71 Stephen Frosh, *Sexual Difference: Masculinity and Psychoanalysis* (London: Routledge, 1994).

Chapter 3

1 Clive Glaser, *Bo-Tsotsi: The Youth Gangs of Soweto, 1935–1976* (London: Heinemann Educational Books, 2000).

2 Steve Mokwena, 'The Era of the Jackrollers: Contextualising the Rise of Youth Gangs in Soweto' (paper presented at the Centre for the Study of Violence and Reconciliation, Johannesburg, 30 October 1991).

3 Monique Marks, *Young Warriors: Youth Politics, Identity and Violence in South Africa* (Johannesburg: Wits University Press, 2002); Mokwena, 'The Era of the Jackrollers'.

4 Most of these youth leaders were young men, as women were excluded from the position of political leadership due to the patriarchal and sexist attitudes that existed at that time.

5 Jacob Dlamini, *Askari: A Story of Collaboration and Betrayal in the Anti-Apartheid Struggle* (Johannesburg: Jacana Media, 2016); Marks, *Young Warriors*; Mokwena, 'The Era of the Jackrollers'.

6 Malose Langa and Gillian Eagle, 'The Intractability of Militarised Masculinity: A Case Study of Former Self-Defence Unit Members in the Kathorus Area, South Africa', *South African Journal of Psychology* 38 (2008); Thokozani Xaba, 'Masculinity and its Malcontents: The Confrontation between "Struggle Masculinity" and "Post-Struggle Masculinity" (1990–1997)', in *Changing Men in Southern Africa*, ed. Robert Morrell (Pietermaritzburg: University of Natal Press, 2001).

7 Langa and Eagle, 'Militarised Masculinity'.

8 Dlamini, *Askari*; Monique Marks and Penny Mckenzie. 'Political Pawns or Social Agents? A Look at Militarised Youth in South Africa.' (Paper presented at the Confronting Crime Conference, Cape Town, September 1995); Raymond Suttner, *The ANC Underground in South Africa* (Johannesburg: Jacana Media, 2008).

9 Langa and Eagle, 'Militarised Masculinity'.

10 Philip Lewis Bonner and Noor Nieftagodien, *Alexandra: A History* (Johannesburg: Wits University Press, 2008).

11 Connell, *Masculinities*.

12 Glaser, *Bo-Tsotsi*.

13 Bonner, and Nieftagodien *Alexandra*.

14 All of the boys/young men whose photographs are reproduced in the book gave me their permission to do so. For reasons of anonymity, however, they are not individually credited.

Chapter 4

1 Wessel van den Berg and Tawanda Makusha, *State of South Africa's Fathers 2018* (Cape Town: Sonke Gender Justice & Human Sciences Research Council,

2018); Linda Richter, Jeremiah Chikovore and Tawanda Makusha, 'The Status of Fatherhood and Fathering in South Africa,' *Childhood Education* 6 (2010).

2 Sharlene Swartz and Arvin Bhana, *Teenage Tata: Voices of Young Fathers in South Africa* (Cape Town: HSRC Press, 2009); Athena Enderstein and Floretta Boonzaaier. 'Narratives of Young South African Fathers: Redefining Masculinity through Fatherhood. *Journal of Gender Studies* 24 (2015.)

3 All the names used in this book are pseudonyms to protect the identities of the participants in the research project.

4 William S Pollack, *Real Boys: Rescuing Our Sons from the Myths* (New York: Random House, 1998).

5 Eddy Mazembo Mavungu, Hayley Thomson-de Boor and Karabo Mphaka, *So We Are ATM Fathers: A Study of Absent Fathers in Johannesburg, South Africa* (Johannesburg: Centre for Social Development in Africa, University of Johannesburg and Sonke Gender Justice, 2013.)

6 Mavungu, Thomson-de Boor and Mphaka, *So We Are ATM Fathers*.

7 Michael J Diamond, 'The Shaping of Masculinity: Revisioning Boys Turning Away from Their Mothers to Construct Male Gender Identity,' *The International Journal of Psychoanalysis* 85 (2005).

8 Motlalepule Nathane-Taulela and Mzikazi Nduna, 'Young Women's Experiences Following Discovering a Biological Father in Mpumalanga Province, South Africa,' *Open Family Studies Journal* 6 (2014).

9 Lacan, *Complexes Familiaux*.

Chapter 5

1 Simon Howell and Louise Vincent. '"Licking the Snake" – the i'Khothane and Contemporary Township Youth Identities in South Africa,' *South African Review of Sociology* 45, 2 (2014); Ellen, Hurst, 'Tsotsitaal, Global Culture and Local Style: Identity and Recontextualisation in Twenty-First Century South African Townships', *Social Dynamics* 35, 2 (2009); Nadine Dolby, 'Youth and the Global Popular: The Politics and Practices of Race in South Africa,' *European Journal of Cultural Studies* 2 (1999); Nadine Dolby, 'The Shifting Ground of Race: The Role of Taste in Youth's Production of Identities,' *Race Ethnicity and Education* 3 (2000); Selikow, Zulu and Cedras, 'The Ingagara, the Regte and the Cherry'; Garth Stevens and Rafiq Lockhart, '"Coca-Cola Kids" – Reflections on Black Adolescent Identity Development in Post-Apartheid South Africa,' *South African Journal of Psychology* 27 (1997).

2 Frosh, Phoenix and Pattman, *Young Masculinities*.

3 Patrick Burton and Lezanne Leoschut, *School Violence in South Africa: Results of 2012 National School Violence Survey* (Cape Town: Centre for Justice and Crime

Prevention, 2013); Patrick Burton, *Merchants, Skollies, and Stones: Experiences of School Violence in South Africa* (Cape Town: Centre for Justice and Crime Prevention, 2008); Vusumzi Ncontsa and Almon Shumba, 'The Nature, Causes and Effects of School Violence in South African High Schools,' *South African Journal of Education* 33, 3 (2013).

4   Burton and Leoschut, *School Violence in South Africa*; Burton, *Merchants, Skollies, and Stones*; Ncontsa and Shumba, 'The Nature, Causes and Effects.'

5   Whitehead, 'Man to Man Violence'.

6   Burton, *Merchants, Skollies, and Stones*; Ncontsa and Shumba, 'The Nature, Causes and Effects.'

7   Duncan Cartwright, *Psychoanalysis, Violence and Rage-Type Murder: Murdering Minds* (New York: Routledge, 2014).

8   Rosine Jozef Perelberg, *Psychoanalytic Understanding of Violence and Suicide* (London: Routledge, 1999); Mary Target and Peter Fonagy, 'Fathers in Modern Psychoanalysis and in Society: The Role of the Father and Child Development' in *The Importance of Fathers: The Psychoanalytic Re-Evaluation*, ed. Judith Trowell and Alicia Etchegoyen (London: Routledge, 2002).

9   Barker, *Dying to Be Men*; Bhana, 'Violence and the Gendered Negotiation'.

10 Barker, *Dying to Be Men*; Bhana, 'Violence and the Gendered Negotiation'.

11 Frosh, Phoenix and Pattman, *Young Masculinities*.

12 Wayne Martino and Maria Pallotta-Chiarolli, *So What's a Boy? Addressing Issues of Masculinity and Schooling* (Maidenhead: Open University Press, 2003).

13 Diane Reay, 'Troubling, Troubled and Troublesome? Working with Boys in the Primary School' in *Boys and Girls in the Primary Classroom*, ed. Christine Skelton and Becky Francis, 151–161 (Buckingham: Open University Press, 2003).

14 Martino and Pallotta-Chiarolli, *So What's a Boy?*; Bhana, 'Violence and the Gendered Negotiation'.

15 Martino and Pallotta-Chiarolli, *So What's a Boy?*

Chapter 6

1   Selikow, Zulu and Cedras. 'The Ingagara, the Regte and the Cherry'.

2   Connell, *Masculinities*; Segal, *Slow Motion*.

3   Chris Dolan, 'Collapsing Masculinities and Weak States: A Case Study of Northern Uganda,' in *Masculinities Matter! Men, Gender and Development*, ed. Frances Cleaver (London: Zed Books, 2002); Tamara Shefer and Nyameka Mankayi, 'The (Hetero)Sexualization of the Military and the Militarization of (Hetero)Sex: Discourses on Male (Hetero)Sexual Practices among a Group of Young Men in the South African Military,' *Sexualities* 10, 2 (2007).

4 Candida Yates, 'Masculinity and Good Enough Jealousy,' *Psychoanalytic Studies* 2 (2000).

5 Deevia Bhana and Bronwynne Anderson, 'Desire and Constraint in the Construction of South African Teenage Women's Sexualities,' *Sexualities* 16 (2013).

6 Mindy Stombler, '"Buddies" or "Slutties": The Collective Sexual Reputation of Fraternity Little Sisters,' *Gender and Society* 8 (1994).

7 Wood and Jewkes, 'Dangerous Love'.

8 Elmien Lesch and Lou-Marie Kruger, 'Reflections on the Sexual Agency of Young Women in a Low-Income Rural South African Community,' *South African Journal of Psychology* 34 (2004): 464-86; Bhana and Anderson, 'Desire and Constraint'.

9 Jane M Ussher, *Body Talk: The Material and Discursive Regulation of Sexuality, Madness, and Reproduction* (New York: Routledge, 1997).

10 Catherine Campbell and Catherine MacPhail, 'Peer Education, Gender and the Development of Critical Consciousness: Participatory HIV Prevention by South African Youth,' *Social Science & Medicine* 55 (2002); Deevia Bhana, '"They've Got All the Knowledge": HIV Education, Gender and Sexuality in South African Primary Schools,' *British Journal of Sociology of Education* 30, 2 (2009); Rachel Jewkes and Robert Morrell, 'Sexuality and the Limits of Agency among South African Teenage Women: Theorising Femininities and Their Connections to HIV Risk Practices,' *Social Science & Medicine* 74 (2012).

11 Nigel Edley and Margaret Wetherell, 'Jekyll and Hyde: Men's Constructions of Feminism and Feminists,' *Feminism and Psychology* 11 (2001).

12 Joan Abbott-Chapman and Carey Denholm, 'Adolescents' Risk Activities, Risk Hierarchies and the Influence of Religiosity,' *Journal of Youth Studies* 4 (2001).

13 Janet Holland, Caroline Ramazanoglu, Sue Sharpe and Rachel Thomson, 'Deconstructing Virginity – Young People's Accounts of First Sex,' *Sexual and Relationship Therapy* 15 (2000).

Chapter 7

1 When the terms 'gay' and 'straight' are put in inverted commas in this chapter it is to acknowledge that they are social constructs which the boys used to categorise and label each other.

2 The term 'homosexuality' is used in the book to highlight the participants' views. The researcher is fully aware of negative connotations associated with the use of the term.

3 Whitehead, 'Man to Man Violence'.

4 Cheri J Pascoe, *Dude, You're a Fag: Masculinity and Sexuality in High School* (Los Angeles: University of California Press, 2007).

5 Frosh, Phoenix and Pattman, *Young Masculinities*; Pascoe, *Dude, You're a Fag*.

6 Pascoe, *Dude, You're a Fag*.

7 Deevia Bhana, 'Understanding and Addressing Homophobia in Schools: A View from Teachers,' *South African Journal of Education* 32 (2012); Deevia Bhana, '"Managing" the Rights of Gays and Lesbians: Reflections from Some South African Secondary Schools,' *Education, Citizenship and Social Justice* 9 (2014).

8 Neil Henderson and Tamara Shefer, 'Practices of Power and Abuse in Gay Male Relationships: An Exploratory Case Study of a Young, isiXhosa-Speaking Man in the Western Cape, South Africa,' *South African Journal of Psychology* 38 (2008); Finn Reygan and Ashley Lynette, 'Heteronormativity, Homophobia and "Culture" Arguments in KwaZulu-Natal, South Africa,' *Sexualities* 17 (2014).

9 Neil Henderson, "Top, Bottom, Versatile": Narratives of Sexual Practices in Gay Relationships in the Cape Metropole, South Africa,' *Culture, Health & Sexuality* 20 (2018).

10 S Rankotha, 'How Black Men Involved in Same-Sex Relationships Construct Their Masculinities,' in *Performing Queer: Shaping Sexualities 1994–2004*, ed. Mikkie van Zyl and Melissa Steyn, 165–175. Cape Town: Kwela, 2005.

11 Butler, *Gender Trouble*.

12 Butler, *Gender Trouble*.

13 Pascoe, *Dude, You're a Fag*.

Chapter 8

1 Catriona Macleod and Tracey Feltham-King, 'Young Pregnant Women and Public Health: Introducing a Critical Reparative Justice/Care Approach Using South African Case Studies,' *Critical Public Health* 2 (2019); Monde D Makiwane, Linda Richter and Lizette Philips-Reynard, *An Investigation of the Link between Social Grants and Teenage Pregnancy* (Cape Town: HSRC Press, 2006).

2 Swartz and Bhana, *Teenage Tata*; Robert Morrell, Deevia Bhana and Tamara Shefer, *Books and Babies: Pregnancy and Young Parents in Schools* (Cape Town: HSRC Press, 2012); Deevia Bhana and Nomvuyo Nkani, 'When African Teenagers Become Fathers: Culture, Materiality and Masculinity,' *Culture, Health & Sexuality* 16, 4 (2014).

3 Morrell, Bhana and Shefer, *Books and Babies*; Swartz and Bhana, *Teenage Tata*; Bhana and Nkani, 'When African Teenagers Become Fathers.'

4 Swartz and Bhana, *Teenage Tata*.

5 Mark Hunter, 'Cultural Politics and Masculinities: Multiple-Partners in Historical Perspective in KwaZulu-Natal' in *Men Behaving Differently*, ed. Graeme Reid and Liz Walker, 139–60 (Cape Town: Double Storey, 2005); Swartz and Bhana, *Teenage Tata*.

6   Dorrit Posel and Stephanie Rudwick, 'Marriage and Bridewealth (Ilobolo) in Contemporary Zulu Society,' *African Studies Review* 57 (2014).

7   Swartz and Bhana, *Teenage Tata.*

8   Jay Fagan and Elisa Bernd, 'Adolescent Fathers' Parenting Stress, Social Support, and Involvement with Infants,' *Journal of Research on Adolescence* 17 (2007).

9   Grace Khunou, 'Money and Gender Relations in the South African Maintenance System,' *South African Review of Sociology* 43 (2012); Grace Khunou, 'Fathers Don't Stand a Chance: Experiences of Custody, Access, and Maintenance' in *Baba: Men and Fatherhood in South Africa*, ed. Linda Richter and Robert Morrell (Cape Town: HSRC Press, 2006).

10 Khunou, 'Money and Gender Relations.'

11 Mavungu, Thomson-de Boor and Mphaka, *So We Are ATM Fathers.*

12 bell hooks, *The Will to Change: Men, Masculinity, and Love* (New York: Washington Square Press, 2004).

Chapter 9

1   Nhlanhla Mkhize, 'African Traditions and the Social, Economic and Moral Dimensions of Fatherhood,' in *Baba: Men and Fatherhood in South Africa*, ed. Linda Richter and Robert Morrell (Cape Town: HSRC Press, 2006).

2   Target and Fonagy, 'Fathers in Modern Psychoanalysis and in Society.'

3   Diamond, 'Shaping of Masculinity'.

4   Peter Blos, *Son and Father: Before and Beyond the Oedipus Complex* (New York: Free Press, 1985).

5   Barker, *Dying to Be Men.*

6   Abbott-Chapman and Denholm, 'Adolescents' Risk Activities.'

7   Marie Rosenkrantz Lindegaard and Sasha Gear, 'Violence Makes Safe in South African Prisons: Prison Gangs, Violent Acts, and Victimization among Inmates,' *Focaal* 2014 (2014); Jonny Steinberg, *The Number: One Man's Search for Identity in the Cape Underworld and Prison Gangs* (Johannesburg: Jonathan Ball Publishers, 2004).

Bibliography

Abbott-Chapman, Joan and Carey Denholm. 'Adolescents' Risk Activities, Risk Hierarchies and the Influence of Religiosity.' *Journal of Youth Studies* 4 (2001): 279–97.

Anderson, Eric. *Inclusive Masculinity: The Changing Nature of Masculinities.* New York: Routledge, 2010.

Attwell, Pamela Ann. 'Real Boys: Concepts of Masculinity among School Teachers.' MA dissertation, University of Natal, 2002.

Barker, Gary. *Dying to Be Men: Youth, Masculinity and Social Exclusion.* London: Routledge, 2005.

Barker, Gary and Christine Ricardo. *Young Men and the Construction of Masculinity in Sub-Saharan Africa: Implications for HIV/AIDS, Conflict, and Violence.* Washington, DC: World Bank, 2005.

Bhana, Deevia. 'Violence and the Gendered Negotiation of Masculinity among Young Black School Boys in South Africa.' In *African Masculinities: Men in Africa from the Late 19th Century to the Present,* edited by Lahoucine Ouzgane and Robert Morrell. Pietermaritzburg: University of KwaZulu-Natal Press; New York: Palgrave Macmillan, 2005.

Bhana, Deevia. 'What Matters to Girls and Boys in a Black Primary School in South Africa.' *Early Child Development and Care* 175 (2005): 99–111.

Bhana, Deevia. '"They've Got All the Knowledge": HIV Education, Gender and Sexuality in South African Primary Schools.' *British Journal of Sociology of Education* 30, 2 (2009): 165–77.

Bhana, Deevia. 'Understanding and Addressing Homophobia in Schools: A View from Teachers.' *South African Journal of Education* 32 (2012): 307–18.

Bhana, Deevia. '"Managing" the Rights of Gays and Lesbians: Reflections from Some South African Secondary Schools.' *Education, Citizenship and Social Justice* 9 (2014): 67–80.

Bhana, Deevia and Nomvuyo Nkani. 'When African Teenagers Become Fathers: Culture, Materiality and Masculinity.' *Culture, Health & Sexuality* 16, 4 (2014): 337–50.

Bhana, Deevia and Bronwynne Anderson. 'Desire and Constraint in the Construction of South African Teenage Women's Sexualities.' *Sexualities* 16 (2013): 548–64.

Bhana, Deevia and Rob Pattman. 'Girls Want Money, Boys Want Virgins: The Materiality of Love amongst South African Township Youth in the Context of HIV and AIDS.' *Culture, Health & Sexuality* 13 (2011): 961–72.

Biko, Steve. *I Write What I Like: Selected Writings.* Chicago: University of Chicago Press, 2015.

Blos, Peter. *Son and Father: Before and Beyond the Oedipus Complex.* New York: Free Press, 1985.

Bonner, Philip Lewis and Noor Nieftagodien. *Alexandra: A History.* Johannesburg: Wits University Press, 2008.

Bourdieu, Pierre. *Distinction: A Social Critique of the Judgement of Taste.* London: Routledge, 2013.

Brittan, Arthur. *Masculinity and Power.* Oxford: Basil Blackwell, 1989.

Britton, Dana M. 'Homophobia and Homosociality: An Analysis of Boundary Maintenance.' *The Sociological Quarterly* 31 (1990): 423–39.

Bruce, David. 'Danger, Threats or Just Fear.' *SA Crime Quarterly* 13 (2005): 23–8.

Burton, Patrick. *Merchants, Skollies, and Stones: Experiences of School Violence in South Africa.* Cape Town: Centre for Justice and Crime Prevention, 2008.

Burton, Patrick and Lezanne Leoschut. *School Violence in South Africa: Results of 2012 National School Violence Survey.* Cape Town: Centre for Justice and Crime Prevention, 2013.

Butler, Judith. *Gender Trouble: Feminism and the Subversion of Identity.* New York: Routledge, 1990.

Campbell, Catherine. *Township Families and Youth Identity: The Family's Influence on the Social Identity of Township Youth in a Rapidly Changing South Africa.* Pretoria: Human Sciences Research Council, 1994.

Campbell, Catherine. 'Migrancy, Masculine Identities and AIDS: The Psychosocial Context of HIV Transmission on the South African Gold Mines.' *Social Science & Medicine* 45 (1997): 273–81.

Campbell, Catherine and Catherine MacPhail. 'Peer Education, Gender and the Development of Critical Consciousness: Participatory HIV Prevention by South African Youth.' *Social Science & Medicine* 55 (2002): 331–45.

Carabí, Àngels and Josep Armengol. *Alternative Masculinities for a Changing World.* New York: Palgrave Macmillan, 2014.

Cartwright, Duncan. *Psychoanalysis, Violence and Rage-Type Murder: Murdering Minds.* New York: Routledge, 2014.

Cock, Jacklyn. 'Gun Violence as an Issue of Community Psychology in Contemporary South Africa.' In *Community Psychology Theory, Method and Practice: South African and Other Perspectives,* edited by Mohammed Seedat,

Norman Duncan and Sandy Lazarus, 293–306. Cape Town: Oxford University Press, 2001.

Connell, Raewyn W. *Masculinities.* Cambridge: Polity Press, 1995.

Connell, Raewyn W. *The Men and the Boys.* Cambridge: Polity Press, 2000.

Connell, Raewyn W. *The Role of Men and Boys in Achieving Gender Equality.* Brazil: United Nations, Division for the Advancement of Women, 2003.

Connell, Raewyn W. 'Hegemonic Masculinity: Rethinking the Concept.' *Gender and Society* 19 (2005): 829–59.

CSVR (Centre for the Study of Violence and Reconciliation). *The Violent Nature of Crime in South Africa.* Johannesburg: CSVR, 2009.

Demetriou, Demetrakis. 'Connell's Concept of Hegemonic Masculinity: A Critique.' *Theory and Society* 30 (2001): 337–61.

Diamond, Michael J. 'The Shaping of Masculinity: Revisioning Boys Turning Away from Their Mothers to Construct Male Gender Identity.' *The International Journal of Psychoanalysis* 85 (2005): 359–80.

Dlamini, Jacob. *Askari: A Story of Collaboration and Betrayal in the Anti-Apartheid Struggle.* Johannesburg: Jacana Media, 2016.

Dolan, Chris. 'Collapsing Masculinities and Weak States: A Case Study of Northern Uganda.' In *Masculinities Matter! Men, Gender and Development,* edited by Frances Cleaver, 57–79. London: Zed Books, 2002.

Dolby, Nadine. 'Youth and the Global Popular: The Politics and Practices of Race in South Africa.' *European Journal of Cultural Studies* 2 (1999): 291–309.

Dolby, Nadine. 'The Shifting Ground of Race: The Role of Taste in Youth's Production of Identities.' *Race, Ethnicity and Education* 3 (2000): 7–23.

Donaldson, Mike. 'What Is Hegemonic Masculinity?' *Theory and Society* 22 (1993): 643–57.

Edley, Nigel and Margaret Wetherell. 'Jekyll and Hyde: Men's Constructions of Feminism and Feminists.' *Feminism and Psychology* 11 (2001): 439–57.

Elliot, Anthony. *Concepts of Self.* Cambridge: Polity Press, 2001.

Enderstein, Athena and Floretta Boonzaaier. 'Narratives of Young South African Fathers: Redefining Masculinity through Fatherhood.' *Journal of Gender Studies* 24 (2015): 512–27.

Evans, Meredith, Kathryn Risher, Nompumelelo Zungu, Olive Shisana, Sizulu Moyo, David D Celentano, Brendan Maughan-Brown and Thomas M Rehle. 'Age-Disparate Sex and HIV Risk for Young Women from 2002 to 2012 in South Africa.' *Journal of the International AIDS Society* 19 (2016). Accessed 19 July 2018. Doi: 10.7448/IAS.19.1.21310

Fagan, Jay and Elisa Bernd. 'Adolescent Fathers' Parenting Stress, Social Support, and Involvement with Infants.' *Journal of Research on Adolescence* 17 (2007): 1–22.

Frosh, Stephen. *The Politics of Psychoanalysis: An Introduction to Freud and Post-Freudian Theory.* New York: New York Press, 1999.

Frosh, Stephen. *Sexual Difference: Masculinity and Psychoanalysis.* London: Routledge, 1994.

Frosh, Stephen and Lisa Baraitser. 'Psychoanalysis and Psychosocial Studies.' *Psychoanalysis, Culture & Society* 13 (2008): 346–65.

Frosh, Stephen, Ann Phoenix and Rob Pattman. *Young Masculinities: Understanding Boys in Contemporary Society.* New York: Palgrave, 2002.

Frosh, Stephen, Ann Phoenix and Rob Pattman. 'Taking a Stand: Using Psychoanalysis to Explore the Positioning of Subjects in Discourse.' *British Journal of Social Psychology* 42 (2003): 39–53.

Gender Links. *Research: Gender Violence 'a Reality in South Africa.'* Johannesburg: Gender Links, 2012.

Gilbert, Rob and Pam Gilbert. *Masculinity Goes to School.* Sydney: Allen & Unwin, 1998.

Glaser, Clive. *Bo-Tsotsi: The Youth Gangs of Soweto, 1935–1976.* London: Heinemann Educational Books, 2000.

Gould, Chandre. 'Beaten Bad: The Life Stories of Violent Offenders.' Institute for Security Studies Monographs (2015): 1–144.

Gqola, Pumla Dineo. *Rape: A South African Nightmare.* Johannesburg: Jacana Media, 2016.

Gramsci, Antonio. *Selections from the Prison Notebooks.* New York: International Publishers, 1971.

Haywood, Christian and Máirtín Mac an Ghaill. 'Schooling Masculinities.' In *Understanding Masculinities: Social Relations and Cultural Arenas,* edited by Máirtín Mac an Ghaill, 50–60. Buckingham: Open University Press (1996).

Henderson, Neil. '"Top, Bottom, Versatile": Narratives of Sexual Practices in Gay Relationships in the Cape Metropole, South Africa.' *Culture, Health & Sexuality* 20 (2018): 1145–56.

Henderson, Neil and Tamara Shefer. 'Practices of Power and Abuse in Gay Male Relationships: An Exploratory Case Study of a Young, isiXhosa-Speaking Man in the Western Cape, South Africa.' *South African Journal of Psychology* 38 (2008): 1–20.

Henriques, Julian, Wendy Hollway, Cathy Urwin, Couze Venn and Valerie Walkerdine. *Changing the Subject: Psychology, Social Regulation, and Subjectivity.* New York: Psychology Press, 1998.

Holland, Janet, Caroline Ramazanoglu, Sue Sharpe and Rachel Thomson. 'Deconstructing Virginity – Young People's Accounts of First Sex.' *Sexual and Relationship Therapy* 15 (2000): 221–32.

Hollway, Wendy. *Subjectivity and Method in Psychology: Gender, Meaning and Science.* London: Sage Publications, 1989.

hooks, bell. *The Will to Change: Men, Masculinity, and Love.* New York: Washington Square Press, 2004.

Howell, Simon and Louise Vincent. '"Licking the Snake" – The I'Khothane and Contemporary Township Youth Identities in South Africa.' *South African Review of Sociology* 45, 2 (2014): 60–77.

Hunter, Mark. 'Masculinities, Multiple-Sexual-Partners and AIDS: The Making and Unmaking of Isoka in KwaZulu-Natal.' *Transformation: Critical Perspectives on Southern Africa* 54 (2004): 123–53.

Hunter, Mark. 'Cultural Politics and Masculinities: Multiple-Partners in Historical Perspective in KwaZulu-Natal'. In *Men Behaving Differently*, edited by Graeme Reid and Liz Walker, 139–60. Cape Town: Double Storey, 2005.

Hurst, Ellen. 'Tsotsitaal, Global Culture and Local Style: Identity and Recontextualisation in Twenty-First Century South African Townships, *Social Dynamics* 35, 2 (2009): 244–57.

Institute for Security Studies. 'So Why Do the Numbers Keep Rising? A Reflection on Efforts to Prevent and Respond to Domestic Violence and Rape.' Paper presented at the Institute for Security Studies Seminar, Pretoria, 27 October 2011.

Jensen, Steffen. *Gangs, Politics and Dignity in Cape Town.* Johannesburg: Wits University Press, 2008.

Jewkes, Rachel K, Kristin Dunkle, Mzikazi Nduna and Nwabisa Shai. 'Intimate Partner Violence, Relationship Power Inequity, and Incidence of HIV Infection in Young Women in South Africa: A Cohort Study.' *The Lancet* 376 (2010): 41–8.

Jewkes, Rachel, Michael Flood and James Lang. 'From Work with Men and Boys to Changes of Social Norms and Reduction of Inequities in Gender Relations: A Conceptual Shift in Prevention of Violence against Women and Girls.' *The Lancet* 385 (2015): 1580–89.

Jewkes, Rachel and Robert Morrell. 'Sexuality and the Limits of Agency among South African Teenage Women: Theorising Femininities and Their Connections to HIV Risk Practices.' *Social Science & Medicine* 74 (2012): 1729–37.

Joseph, Stephen and P Alex Linley. 'Growth Following Adversity: Theoretical Perspectives and Implications for Clinical Practice.' *Clinical Psychology Review* 26 (2006): 1041–53.

Khunou, Grace. 'Fathers Don't Stand a Chance: Experiences of Custody, Access, and Maintenance.' In *Baba: Men and Fatherhood in South Africa*, edited by Linda Richter and Robert Morrell, 265–77. Cape Town: HSRC Press, 2006.

Khunou, Grace. 'Money and Gender Relations in the South African Maintenance System.' *South African Review of Sociology* 43 (2012): 4–22.

Khunwane, Mamakiri Nomina. 'Exploring the Perceptions of Sexual Abstinence amongst a Group of Young Black Male Students.' MA dissertation, University of the Witwatersrand, 2008.

Kimmel, Michael. 'Why Men Should Support Gender Equity.' *Women's Studies* 103 (2005): 102–14.

Kimmel, Michael. *Guyland: The Perilous World Where Boys Become Men*. New York: HarperCollins, 2008.

Kimmel, Michael S, Jeff Hearn and Robert W Connell. *Handbook of Studies on Men and Masculinities*. Thousand Oaks: Sage Publications, 2005.

Kimmel, Michael S and Michael A Messner. *Men's Lives*. New York: Pearson Education, 2004.

Kinness, Irvin. *From Urban Street Gangs to Criminal Empires: The Changing Face of Gangs in the Western Cape*. Pretoria: Institute for Security Studies, 2000.

Lacan, Jacques. *Les Complexes Familiaux (Family Complexes)*. Paris: Seuil, 1984.

Langa, Malose. 'Vulnerable Communities: Former Combatants in South Africa.' In *Community Psychology: Analysis, Context and Action*, edited by Norman Duncan, Brett Bowman, Anthony Naidoo, Jace Pillay and Vera Roos, 262–79. Pretoria: Juta, 2007.

Langa, Malose. 'Working with Juvenile Offenders: An Evaluation of Trauma Group Intervention.' *African Safety Promotion: A Journal of Injury and Violence Prevention* 5 (2007): 63–83.

Langa, Malose and Gillian Eagle. 'The Intractability of Militarised Masculinity: A Case Study of Former Self-Defence Unit Members in the Kathorus Area, South Africa.' *South African Journal of Psychology* 38 (2008): 152–75.

Lemanski, Charlotte. 'A New Apartheid? The Spatial Implications of Fear of Crime in Cape Town, South Africa.' *Environment and Urbanization* 16 (2004): 101–12.

Lesch, Elmien and Lou-Marie Kruger. 'Reflections on the Sexual Agency of Young Women in a Low-Income Rural South African Community.' *South African Journal of Psychology* 34 (2004): 464–86.

Lindegaard, Marie Rosenkrantz and Sasha Gear. 'Violence Makes Safe in South African Prisons: Prison Gangs, Violent Acts, and Victimization among Inmates.' *Focaal* 2014 (2014): 35–54.

Macleod, Catriona. 'The Risk of Phallocentrism in Masculinities Studies: How a Revision of the Concept of Patriarchy May Help.' *Psychology in Society* 35 (2007): 4–14.

Macleod, Catriona and Tracey Feltham-King. 'Young Pregnant Women and Public Health: Introducing a Critical Reparative Justice/Care Approach Using South African Case Studies.' *Critical Public Health* (2019): 1–11.

Makiwane, Monde D, Linda Richter and Lizette Philips-Reynard. *An Investigation of the Link between Social Grants and Teenage Pregnancy*. Cape Town: HSRC Press, 2006.

Marks, Monique. *Young Warriors: Youth Politics, Identity and Violence in South Africa*. Johannesburg: Wits University Press, 2002.

Marks, Monique and Penny Mckenzie. 'Political Pawns or Social Agents? A Look at Militarised Youth in South Africa.' Paper presented at the Confronting Crime Conference, Cape Town, September 1995.

Martino, Wayne. '"Cool Boys", "Party Animals", "Squids" and "Poofters": Interrogating the Dynamics and Politics of Adolescent Masculinities in School.' *British Journal of Sociology of Education* 20 (1999): 239–63.

Martino, Wayne and Maria Pallotta-Chiarolli. *So What's a Boy? Addressing Issues of Masculinity and Schooling.* Maidenhead: Open University Press, 2003.

Mavungu, Eddy Mazembo, Hayley Thomson-de Boor and Karabo Mphaka. *So We Are ATM Fathers: A Study of Absent Fathers in Johannesburg, South Africa.* Johannesburg: Centre for Social Development in Africa, University of Johannesburg and Sonke Gender Justice, 2013.

Mkhize, Nhlanhla. 'African Traditions and the Social, Economic and Moral Dimensions of Fatherhood.' In *Baba: Men and Fatherhood in South Africa,* edited by Linda Richter and Robert Morrell, 183–200. Cape Town: HSRC Press, 2006.

Mokwena, Steve. 'The Era of the Jackrollers: Contextualising the Rise of Youth Gangs in Soweto.' Paper presented at the Centre for the Study of Violence and Reconciliation, Johannesburg, 30 October 1991.

Moller, Michael. 'Exploiting Patterns: A Critique of Hegemonic Masculinity.' *Journal of Gender Studies* 16 (2007): 263–76.

Morrell, Robert. *Changing Men in Southern Africa.* Pietermaritzburg: University of Natal Press, 2001.

Morrell, Robert. 'Men, Masculinities and Gender Politics in South Africa: A Reply to Macleod.' *Psychology in Society* 35 (2007): 15–25.

Morrell, Robert, Deevia Bhana and Tamara Shefer. *Books and Babies: Pregnancy and Young Parents in Schools.* Cape Town: HSRC Press, 2012.

Morrell, Robert, Rachel Jewkes and Graham Lindegger. 'Hegemonic Masculinity/ Masculinities in South Africa.' *Culture, Power, and Gender Politics* 15 (2012): 11–30.

MRC (Medical Research Council). 'What Are the Top Causes of Death in South Africa?' Medical Research Council, 2015. Accessed January 2018. http://Www.Mrc.Ac.Za/Bod/Faqdeath.Htm

Nathane-Taulela, Motlalepule and Mzikazi Nduna. 'Young Women's Experiences Following Discovering a Biological Father in Mpumalanga Province, South Africa.' *Open Family Studies Journal* 6 (2014): 62–8.

Ncontsa, Vusumzi and Almon Shumba. 'The Nature, Causes and Effects of School Violence in South African High Schools.' *South African Journal of Education* 33, 3 (2013): 1–15.

Pascoe, Cheri J. *Dude, You're a Fag: Masculinity and Sexuality in High School.* Los Angeles: University of California Press, 2007.

Pease, Bob. 'Reconstructing Masculinity or Ending Manhood? The Potential and Limitations of Transforming Masculine Subjectivities for Gender Equality.' In *Alternative Masculinities for a Changing World,* edited by Àngels Carabí and Josep Armengol, 17–34, New York: Palgrave Macmillan, 2014.

Pease, Bob. 'Men as Allies in Preventing Violence against Women: Principles and Practices for Promoting Accountability.' Center for the Study of Men and Masculinities (2017): 1–32.

Perelberg, Rosine Jozef. *Psychoanalytic Understanding of Violence and Suicide.* London: Routledge, 1999.

Pinnock, Don. *Gang Town.* Cape Town: Tafelberg, 2016.

Pollack, William S. *Real Boys: Rescuing Our Sons from the Myths.* New York: Random House, 1998.

Posel, Dorrit and Stephanie Rudwick. 'Marriage and Bridewealth (Ilobolo) in Contemporary Zulu Society.' *African Studies Review* 57 (2014): 51–72.

Ramphele, Mamphela. *Steering by the Stars: Being Young in South Africa.* Cape Town: Tafelberg, 2002.

Rankotha, S. 'How Black Men Involved in Same-Sex Relationships Construct Their Masculinities.' In *Performing Queer: Shaping Sexualities 1994–2004,* edited by Mikkie van Zyl and Melissa Steyn, 165–75. Cape Town: Kwela, 2005.

Ratele, Kopano. 'Masculinity and Male Mortality in South Africa.' *African Safety Promotion* 6 (2008): 19–41.

Ratele, Kopano. 'Subordinate Black South African Men without Fear.' *Cahiers d'études Africaines* 53 (2013): 247–68.

Ratele, Kopano. *Liberating Masculinities.* Cape Town: HSRC Press, 2016.

Reay, Diane. 'Troubling, Troubled and Troublesome? Working with Boys in the Primary School.' In *Boys and Girls in the Primary Classroom,* edited by Christine Skelton and Becky Francis, 151–61. Buckingham: Open University Press, 2003.

Redpath, Jean, Robert Morrell, Rachel Jewkes and Dean Peacock. *Masculinities and Public Policy in South Africa: Changing Masculinities and Working toward Gender Equality.* Johannesburg: Sonke Gender Justice Network, 2008.

Renold, Emma. '"Other" Boys: Negotiating Non-Hegemonic Masculinities in the Primary School.' *Gender and Education* 16 (2004): 654–63.

Reygan, Finn and Ashley Lynette. 'Heteronormativity, Homophobia and "Culture" Arguments in KwaZulu-Natal, South Africa.' *Sexualities* 17 (2014): 707–23.

Richter, Linda, Jeremiah Chikovore and Tawanda Makusha. 'The Status of Fatherhood and Fathering in South Africa.' *Childhood Education.* 6 (2010): 360–65.

Richter, Linda and Robert Morrell. *Baba: Men and Fatherhood in South Africa.* Cape Town: HSRC Press, 2006.

SACENDU (South African Community Epidemiological Network of Drug Use) (2017).

Salisbury, Jonathan and D Jackson. *Challenging Macho Values: Practical Ways of Working with Adolescent Boys.* London: The Falmer Press, 1996.

Salo, Elaine. 'Social Constructions of Masculinity on the Racial and Gendered Margins of Cape Town.' In *From Boys to Men: Social Constructions of Masculinity in Contemporary Society,* edited by Tamara Shefer, Kopano Ratele, Anna Strebel, Nokuthula Shabalala and Rosemarie Buikema, 160–80. Cape Town: UCT Press, 2007.

Sathiparsad, Reshma. 'Developing Alternative Masculinities as a Strategy to Address Gender-Based Violence.' *International Social Work* 51 (2008): 348–59.

Schapera, Isaac. *Bogwera: Kgatla Initiation.* Mochudi: Phuthadikobo Museum, 1978.

Segal, Lynne. *Slow Motion: Changing Masculinities, Changing Men.* London: Virago, 1990.

Selikow, Terry-Ann, Bheki Zulu and Eugene Cedras. 'The Ingagara, the Regte and the Cherry: HIV/AIDS and Youth Culture in Contemporary Urban Townships.' *Agenda* 17 (2002): 22–32.

Shefer, Tamara and Nyameka Mankayi. 'The(Hetero) Sexualization of the Military and the Militarization of(Hetero) Sex: Discourses on Male(Hetero) Sexual Practices among a Group of Young Men in the South African Military.' *Sexualities* 10, 2 (2007): 189–207.

Shefer, Tamara, Kopano Ratele, Anna Strebel, Nonhlanhla Shabalala and Rosemarie Buikema. *From Boys to Men: Social Constructions of Masculinity in Contemporary Society.* Cape Town: UCT Press, 2007.

Sibanda-Moyo, Nonhlanhla, Eleanor Khonje and Maame Kyerewaa Brobbey. *Violence against Women in South Africa: A Country in Crisis 2017.* Johannesburg: Centre for the Study of Violence and Reconciliation, 2017.

Sigsworth, Romi. *Anyone Can Be a Rapist: An Overview of Sexual Violence in South Africa.* Johannesburg: Centre for the Study of Violence and Reconciliation, 2009.

Steinberg, Jonny. *The Number: One Man's Search for Identity in the Cape Underworld and Prison Gangs.* Johannesburg: Jonathan Ball Publishers, 2004.

Stevens, Garth and Rafiq Lockhart. '"Coca-Cola Kids" – Reflections on Black Adolescent Identity Development in Post-Apartheid South Africa.' *South African Journal of Psychology* 27 (1997): 250–55.

Stombler, Mindy. '"Buddies" or "Slutties": The Collective Sexual Reputation of Fraternity Little Sisters.' *Gender and Society* 8 (1994): 297–323.

Suttner, Raymond. *The ANC Underground in South Africa.* Johannesburg: Jacana Media, 2008.

Swain, Jon. '"The Money's Good, the Fame's Good, the Girls Are Good": The Role of Playground Football in the Construction of Young Boys' Masculinity in a Junior School.' *British Journal of Sociology of Education* 21 (2000): 95–109.

Swain, Jon. 'How Young Schoolboys Become Somebody: The Role of the Body in the Construction of Masculinity.' *British Journal of Sociology of Education* 24 (2003): 299–314.

Swartz, Sharlene and Arvin Bhana. *Teenage Tata: Voices of Young Fathers in South Africa.* Cape Town: HSRC Press, 2009.

Target, Mary and Peter Fonagy. 'Fathers in Modern Psychoanalysis and in Society: The Role of the Father and Child Development.' In *The Importance of Fathers: The Psychoanalytic Re-Evaluation,* edited by Judith Trowell and Alicia Etchegoyen, 45–66. London: Routledge, 2002.

Unterhalter, Elaine. 'Global Inequality, Capabilities, Social Justice: The Millennium Development Goal for Gender Equality in Education.' *International Journal of Educational Development* 25 (2005): 111–22.

Ussher, Jane M. *Body Talk: The Material and Discursive Regulation of Sexuality, Madness, and Reproduction.* New York: Routledge, 1997.

Van den Berg, Wessel and Tawanda Makusha. *State of South Africa's Fathers 2018,* Cape Town: Sonke Gender Justice & Human Sciences Research Council, 2018.

Watson, Anne, Michael Kehler and Wayne Martino. 'The Problem of Boys' Literacy Underachievement: Raising Some Questions.' *Journal of Adolescent and Adult Literacy* 53 (2010): 356–61.

Wetherell, Margaret and Nigel Edley. 'Negotiating Hegemonic Masculinity.' *Feminism and Psychology* 9 (1999): 335–56.

Whitehead, Antony. 'Man to Man Violence: How Masculinity May Work as a Dynamic Risk Factor.' *The Howard Journal of Criminal Justice* 44 (2005): 411–22.

Wood, Katherine and Rachel Jewkes. '"Dangerous" Love: Reflections on Violence amongst Xhosa Township Youth.' In *Changing Men in Southern Africa,* edited by Robert Morrell, 317–35. Pietermaritzburg: University of Natal Press, 2005.

World Health Organization. *Global Status Report on Road Safety 2015.* World Health Organization, 2015.

Xaba, Thokozani. 'Masculinity and its Malcontents: The Confrontation between "Struggle Masculinity" and "Post-Struggle Masculinity" (1990–1997)'. In *Changing Men in Southern Africa,* edited by Robert Morrell, 105–24. Pietermaritzburg: University of Natal Press, 2001.

Yates, Candida. 'Masculinity and Good Enough Jealousy.' *Psychoanalytic Studies* 2 (2000): 1460–70.

Index

The first letters of movements with a hashtag (#) are used for alphabetical ordering. Prepositions are not used for alphabetical ordering.

Printed and bound by CPI Group (UK) Ltd, Croydon, CR0 4YY

13/04/2025

14656580-0003